"Ready to crush your career? Then dive into the pages of Dee Ann Turner's newest book and allow her to guide you from landing the job of your dreams to building a career you love. *Crush Your Career* is full of stories and counsel that will help you navigate your career path no matter where you are right now."

Jon Acuff, *New York Times* bestselling author
of *Finish* and *Soundtracks*

"Jump headfirst into this book, and allow your job to be a platform to fulfill your work and live the life you were meant to live. Dee Ann will guide you in discovering what that is."

from the foreword by Dr. Tim Elmore, founder/CEO
of GrowingLeaders.com

"Quoting Jackie Robinson's remarkably simple but powerful idea 'A life is not important except for the impact it has on other lives,' Turner asks us to think about work through the lens of impact. In ten engaging and practical chapters, each full of insights and examples, she provides advice to help readers see and build careers that foster character and provide more joy in their lives. I recommend it to the young and the not-so-young alike; anyone seeking more fulfilment in their work will find something helpful in this book."

Amy C. Edmondson, professor at Harvard Business School
and author of *The Fearless Organization*

"I vividly remember my awkward first months on the job as a young leader in three different fields: law, radio, and ministry. I so wish I'd had this book then. Dee Ann Turner has written a superbly practical and deeply helpful manual that should be required reading for every young leader. She should know, having developed and trained one of the most respected and admired workforces on the planet."

Carey Nieuwhof, leadership author and podcaster

"Jobs are important because they enable us to make a living. But as Dr. Tim Elmore points out, work is bigger than a job: work is about purpose. Your job is a platform for your work, your calling, the things God made you for. Dee Ann Turner has dedicated her life to helping others find their purpose. Thank you, Dee Ann, for *Crush Your Career*, an encouraging road map leading to truly fulfilling work!"

Dr. Crawford W. Loritts Jr., author of *Leadership as an Identity*
and senior pastor of Fellowship Bible Church, Roswell, Georgia

"I'm often asked how I ended up where I am. Although I'd love to tell you some fantastic story about overnight success, the truth is much less glamorous, involving some mistakes, a lot of hard work, and a bit of chance. But the one secret that contributed to my career more than anything else? A few invested mentors who believed in me and helped me take the next step. Dee Ann Turner has been one of those mentors. And through *Crush Your Career*, she is that mentor for you too. Pull up a seat and get ready to take a lot of notes. You're on your way toward the career you've always dreamed of."

Michele Cushatt, chief training officer of Michael Hyatt & Company, author, and speaker

"This is a must-read guide to getting a job, keeping a job, and growing your career, yourself, and your role no matter where you work or what you do. This book is ideal for anybody starting, reinventing, or trying to supercharge their career going forward. Stay strong, get stronger, and crush your career with Dee Ann's help."

Bruce Tulgan, bestselling author of *The Art of Being Indispensable at Work* and many other books and chairman of RainmakerThinking, Inc.

"In her newest release, Dee Ann Turner has produced the holy grail of information for young adults seeking real success in the business world. *Crush Your Career* is a complete and enjoyable guide to each individual process that produces long-term professional fulfillment. In an area of life so important to so many, this book is in a category of one!"

Andy Andrews, *New York Times* bestselling author of *The Traveler's Gift* and The Noticer series

"Dee Ann has succeeded where so many career books have failed: she has written something that is both extremely practical and a genuine joy to read! If you can't trust the woman who built Chick-fil-A's best-in-class hiring processes for career advice, who *can* you trust? I can't recommend this book highly enough."

Jordan Raynor, national bestselling author of *Called to Create* and *Master of One*

"In a rapidly changing world, it's becoming tougher than ever to land a good job and navigate a career that connects your God-given talents, skills, and passions with work that matters. In *Crush Your Career*, Dee Ann Turner delivers timeless and tested principles that worked in her long career. They can work for you too if you are willing to learn and then use these principles as you navigate work and career opportunities. Wherever you are in your journey, this book is valuable guidance, encouragement, and wisdom to move you forward!"

B. Lynn Chastain, senior vice president and general counsel
of Chick-fil-A, Inc. (Retired)

"As I tell most fellow authors, 'be a painkiller with your book and focus on those pain points you're trying to alleviate.' Dee Ann does just that, and she's hitting a generation with tactical guidance to more effectively pursue their next job. I tell many young people today that 'life should be a ruthless pursuit of passions, but we have to hone our strategies for finding our next job.' What's amazing is Dee Ann Turner does just that while borrowing from her background of building one of the most famous and sought-after cultures in corporate America at Chick-fil-A. This should be mandatory reading for all budding executives."

Chris Tuff, national bestselling author of *The Millennial Whisperer*
and partner at 22Squared

"I can't think of anyone I'd rather have as a guide in my career journey than Dee Ann Turner. *Crush Your Career* reads like you're sitting across the table from a trusted friend and mentor. With stories that both inspire and challenge and with very practical steps to help you navigate the next step you're facing, this book will equip you with the confidence to do just what it promises."

Jenni Catron, founder of the 4Sight Group
and author of *The 4 Dimensions of Extraordinary Leadership*

"Dee Ann Turner selected some of the best talent in the restaurant business during her three decades at Chick-fil-A. Now she teaches talent how to launch and grow a career. Our leadership team loved her previous book, *Bet on Talent*. Our staff is going to love *Crush Your Career*! If you are ready to crush yours, this book is for you!"

Chris Carneal, founder/CEO of Booster

CRUSH YOUR CAREER

ACE THE INTERVIEW, LAND THE JOB, AND LAUNCH YOUR FUTURE

DEE ANN TURNER

BakerBooks

a division of Baker Publishing Group
Grand Rapids, Michigan

Published by Baker Books
a division of Baker Publishing Group
PO Box 6287, Grand Rapids, MI 49516-6287
www.bakerbooks.com

Printed in the United States of America

Library of Congress Cataloging-in-Publication Data
Names: Turner, Dee Ann, author.
Title: Crush your career : ace the interview, land the job, and launch your future / Dee Ann Turner.
Description: Grand Rapids, MI : Baker Books, [2021]
Identifiers: LCCN 2020034730 | ISBN 9780801094378 (cloth)
Subjects: LCSH: Career development. | Job satisfaction. | Job hunting.
Classification: LCC HF5381 .T798 2021 | DDC 650.14—dc23
LC record available at https://lccn.loc.gov/2020034730

Some names and details have been changed to protect the privacy of the individuals involved.

The proprietor is represented by Alive Literary Agency, 7680 Goddard Street, Suite 200, Colorado Springs, CO 80920, www.aliveliterary.com.

21 22 23 24 25 26 27   7 6 5 4 3 2 1

For my mother, **Joyce D. Dailey**,
because she is where my story began.
You role modeled a commitment to core values
and work ethic all of my life and gave me
a foundation on which to build
a career and live the life I love.
Thank you for such a treasured gift.

To all of you reading this book,
finding your path, and writing your own story:
I believe that the generations of leaders
to come will be resilient, innovative, and collaborative
and will meet challenges and solve problems
to move us all forward.

Contents

Contents

Foreword

This book is long overdue.

Dee Ann Turner has created a resource that feels like a life coach who's sitting down with a mug of coffee and offering sound wisdom, one-on-one, to anyone in need of career advice. As I read through it, I could hear Dee Ann speaking, sometimes chuckling, often smiling, and always concerned that we catch an insight so that we don't have to repeat her mistakes.

- She is authentic.
- She is practical.
- She is sound.
- She is relevant and helpful.

I could identify with many of her stories and case studies. She reminded me of my own career journey and the forks in the road I faced along the way. Too many times, people begin their career looking only for a job and neglect to see they have a "work" to accomplish. I believe your work is almost always bigger than your job, and discovering it is what makes your career.

- Your jobs will come and go throughout your career. Your work tends to be the common thread you find in each of those jobs.

- Your job is about earning income, bonuses, and perks. Your work is about what you give back, the contribution you make in your life.
- Your job enables you to make a living. Your work enables you to leave a legacy.

This book is about seeking the right job so you can find your work: the calling you are hardwired to fulfill with your talent and passion. One's about a paycheck; the other's about a purpose. Dee Ann believes the two don't have to be mutually exclusive. I agree. As you allow her to counsel you about your jobs, you're going to find practical, detailed tips for each step of your journey. But don't miss your higher calling. Jump headfirst into this book, and allow your job to be a platform to fulfill your work and live the life you were meant to live. Dee Ann will guide you in discovering what that is. When you do:

- Your supervisor will thank you.
- Your teammates will thank you.
- Your family will thank you.

I've come to believe that people discover their sense of purpose in different ways. Some people appear lucky, figuring out what they want to do very early in life. For others, it happens over time. Following are five examples of what I'm talking about:

1. *Thunderbolt.* These people experience an epiphany about their career and calling. In a moment or a brief season of time, they get it figured out. Those lucky dogs.
2. *Walking through open doors.* These folks only understand bits and pieces, and their understanding unfolds in time. As they walk through an open door, a new one opens.
3. *Call from birth.* For some reason, these individuals figure it out as children. They say things such as "I always knew

I was supposed to be a nurse." Once again, if only we were all so lucky.

4. *Growing awareness.* These people get a general idea for their direction, and as they move toward that sketchy vision, the details get filled in. Clarity comes with time.

5. *Guide on the side.* These individuals gain wisdom and direction from others who know them well or who know how careers work. They have mentors who coach them.

As you may have guessed, most people do not identify with "thunderbolt" and "call from birth." They may wish it was so, but most fall under #2, #4, and #5. They gain wisdom about their gifts, calling, and career over the years and often when mentors enter their lives with wise counsel.

That's the genius behind the "guide on the side."

This is what *Crush Your Career* could be for you—the mentor you've been looking for to help you fill in the blanks. Dee Ann Turner has helped thousands of ordinary people make their life worth living. I recommend her as a mentor for you as well.

Dr. Tim Elmore, founder/CEO, GrowingLeaders.com

Acknowledgments

All thanks be to God, who wrote my story and walked me through it step by step over all of the days of my life.

Thank you to so many people who took this book from just an idea to reality:

Ashley Turner, my incredible husband, who does innumerable and immeasurable tasks to help me succeed and be at my very best. He is the epitome of servant leadership and the great love of my life.

Our sons, who together are the second great loves of my life.

Trey Turner, our youngest son and Gen Z member, who advised me on every idea in this book.

Trevor Turner, our middle son, a great encourager in my life and a willing participant in considering and implementing my coaching.

Trenton Turner, our oldest son, for providing me with needed legal expertise and by virtue of being the firstborn enduring all of our parenting experiments.

Justin Miller, Ashley Baumgardner, and Bethany Swanson, for sharing your stories with me and encouraging my faith in the next generation of leaders.

A host of people who provided me with significant guidance and insight: Lynn Chastain, Holly Moore, Nancy Vespraskas, André Kennebrew, Ed Howie, Jaime Lutz, Matt Chastain, Becky Chin, Becky Pickle, Greg Whittle, Brian Coursey, Cathy Dunn, Cindy Allen, Matthew Sexton, Andrea Bell, Kaitlyn Brooks, Jennifer Bennett, Bing Oliver, George Carden, Ashley Chapman, Polly Williamson, Trahlyta Miller, Holly Morris, Kathy Crockett, Casey Ross, Michelle Cushatt, Jason Young, David Alexander, Alison English, Snowdell Jackson, Kristin Braddy, David Roberts, David Murphy, Heather Dixon Adams, Bill Golden, Hallie Pappas, Holly Duncan, Valerie Bogle, Rhonda Abbey, Lauren McGuire, Kate McNerney, Aimee Dimwiddie, Robin Stanley, Heather Redick, Genia Rogers, Juli Salvagio, Maggie Rheney, Becky Neill, Edgar Cabrera, Alex Vann, Dean Collins, Catherine Jackson, Diana Murphy, Len Hill, and Stacy Bartlett.

All of my clients, who have encouraged me and helped spread my messages of the importance of creating a remarkable culture and selecting extraordinary talent to win the hearts of customers.

The tremendous number of millennials and Gen Z members who helped me ideate and shared the stories in this book.

Devin Lee Duke of Choice Media and Communications for support and encouragement.

The editorial, marketing, and sales staff at Baker Publishing, including Rebekah Guzman, Gisèle Mix, Eileen Hanson, Wendy Wetzel, and Patti Brinks.

Jamie Chavez, who made sure I used the right sources and encouraged me that my own words are sometimes better than those of others in telling my story.

Bryan Norman and the Alive Literary staff.

Introduction

Ceiling and Visibility Unlimited (CAVU)

During the COVID-19 pandemic, the US Air Force Thunderbirds and the US Navy Blue Angels conducted flyovers above hospitals in many cities across the United States to honor the medical personnel waging war on the COVID-19 virus. En route to a local hospital, the majestic planes flew above my home. As they passed over at speeds up to 620 mph against a perfect bright-blue April sky, the term that immediately entered my mind was CAVU.

Until the passing of former US president George H. W. Bush, I had never heard of the acronym *CAVU*. It is an aviator's term that means "ceiling and visibility unlimited." The phrase was a favorite of the forty-first president of the United States, a former naval aviator. For a pilot, CAVU is the most desirable circumstances when flying. Under such conditions, a pilot has clear vision all the way to the horizon. Not only is the view incredible in such circumstances but also navigation is far less complex.

Wouldn't it be wonderful if we could navigate our careers in the spirit of CAVU? When we initially start the search for our first career position, the ceiling and visibility seem unlimited. When our lives are in front of us, even in uncertain times, the future is bright and we can envision success all the way to the horizon of our career. Then reality sets in, and we realize that getting the job we want, keeping the job we love, and growing the career we desire are difficult, even in the best of times. In difficult economic times, the competition for jobs can be fierce, but with belief in ourselves, persistence, and preparation, we can still find our way to career success. It's exciting to embark on a career journey and pursue the work we were made to do. For that moment, there appears to be no ceiling to the possibilities, and the view appears completely clear for as far as we can see.

In reality, every day in the world of work is not CAVU. Even with a great start to a career, somewhere along the way the horizon can become hazy, and fog rolls in to cloud the view. Just like the pilot who must switch from visual navigation to instrumental navigation, we also need navigational aids to help us find our way in the world of work.

We are most successful at navigating anything when we start with a plan for where we want to go. *Crush Your Career* provides a plan for someone who is just beginning to think about a future career as well as someone who is starting over and searching for a guide to chart a course for change. It is intended to be a navigational tool for those trying to find their way into and through a career. It's also a guidebook for the leaders, counselors, advisors, parents, coaches, teachers, and others who will help them and a refresher for all of us on what makes us successful in the workplace.

As a young person, my visibility of the future was limited, though my desire for success was limitless. Mostly due to the influence of my parents, the only path I knew was pursuing professional careers: law, medicine, and education. All of them are very noble, but none of them were in line with a calling that I had not yet even discovered. I found my way through experimenting, collecting wisdom from others, and trying to apply what I learned to my own journey.

From age eight, I wanted to be a writer, but it would take four decades of navigating fog and haze before I realized and fulfilled the dream of becoming an author. In the meantime, I had to find a job, keep a job, and grow a career. It's a reality for most of us. During my first trip to college, I was a journalism major. I left college in the midst of an economic recession, and finding a job in that field was challenging and almost impossible. Additionally, I lacked the life experience at that time to write about anything that readers would find interesting. I accepted my first career position working for a small, family-owned advertising firm. It was less than ideal, but I needed experience, and the way to get experience is to get started. Sometimes it is in the most miserable situations that we learn our most valuable lessons. Such was the case for me.

After numerous interviews, I accepted a job at a firm that was willing to give me a place to start. The high turnover rate should have been a clue that it was an organization with a poor culture, but I didn't ask a lot of questions. This was in the middle of a recession, and jobs were scarce. I needed to start somewhere.

Surviving just eighteen months in the advertising field, I switched careers rather accidentally. In these current times of rapid change and frequent job transitions, it is not unusual at all for people to change jobs every eighteen to twenty-four months. Several decades ago, it was not nearly as common. When I first applied to Chick-fil-A, I was pursuing a position in the advertising department. After enduring a lengthy and intense interviewing process, I was offered and I accepted a job in human resources. All along, I believed and expected that I would eventually return to advertising, but that did not turn out to be my path.

My path became helping others find their paths. Over a thirty-three-year career, I selected thousands of candidates for various positions and roles, many of whom were just beginning their careers. Over that same time period, I led teams and coached staff members and mentees on the principles contained in this book. I helped them navigate their paths to not just a way to make a living but also, and more importantly, to discover a calling in which to make a life. As leaders, it is sometimes easier for us to see potential for the future in others than it is for them to see it in themselves. It is the role of the leader to help others discover their paths.

Over the course of my career, there were many times I needed a book like this one to help me navigate through the fog and haze in the workplace. We spend twenty-two years, on average, preparing to start a career. In primary school, we draw pictures and write stories about what we want to be when we "grow up." As early as middle school, we begin taking assessments and inventories as to our interests and aptitudes. We spend our years in high school preparing to be accepted to the college, university, or technical school that will put us on the path to our first career job.

Landing the first job is a little bit like having a baby. Now that we have it, what do we do with it? This book will help you know what to do in a multitude of situations. However, let me be clear. The expertise in this book was born somewhat of successes but more so in the failures. We learn much more by our mistakes than we do by our successes. I will share with you my successes, but much of what you will read is what I learned from my mistakes.

Finally, the motivation for writing this book is deeply personal. At the time of this writing, along with my husband, I am continuing to coach, counsel, and guide the three twenty-somethings in my life as they find a job, keep a job, and grow their careers. Over countless hours of deep conversations, I listened and advised as they anxiously contemplated their futures. Together, we found answers that helped them on their journeys.

I do not believe for a moment that happiness in life is determined by the forty-plus hours we spend at work each week or by the paycheck we bring home. In fact, after thirty-seven years in the workforce, I am certain it is not. They are only pieces of a much bigger picture. Hopefully, our lives are full of purpose, passion, and people who fulfill our hearts, dreams, and desires. Our professions are the vocational fulfillment of our calling. We are doing the very thing God made us for. However, for most people, making a living is a necessity, and if we are struggling to make one, it will negatively impact all the other areas of our lives.

My hope is that this book will help you to successfully navigate finding a job, keeping a job, and growing a career. I also hope that it will help you to successfully make a living that supports the kind of life you dream of and desire. The goal is not the horizon. We will all arrive there one day. The goal is to arrive fulfilled by the satisfaction of a job well done and a career well served and the mission of a life's work complete. I wish you CAVU as you journey!

GET A JOB

PART I

The memory is vivid to me. From the day I turned fifteen years old, I wanted to get a work permit and find a part-time job. A friend of mine was scooping ice cream at the local Baskin-Robbins ice cream store, and that appeared to me to be the ticket to earn some money and establish my independence. She was making $2.90 an hour, which certainly exceeded the $1 per hour I was making babysitting. I wasn't thinking so much about learning life skills, bolstering my college application, or gaining job skills. Like many teenagers, I only thought about making money to buy the latest fashion, save for a car, and earn money for college. Being surrounded by thirty-one flavors of deliciousness for several hours each week sounded like a pretty good idea too! Ultimately, my parents preferred that I continue doing odd jobs to make spending money so that I would have the opportunity to be fully engaged in school, family, and church activities.

Taking on the responsibility of a first job is one of the most important steps in preparing for a career. My friend, the ice cream scooper, learned to show up on time, in the proper uniform, and with her name badge attached to her apron. Those are basic skills, but they lead to learning how to follow directions, communicate with coworkers and the boss, and respond appropriately to customers. These are the foundational skills that every boss expects when a new staff member joins the team to begin a career.

When we decide it's time to get a job or that it's time for our children to get a job, it's not only to earn money. Far more importantly, it's setting the stage for a successful future career. The choices we make at the beginning often impact what happens in the end.

1

Preparing Your Character

When I was about five years old, my mother taught me my first memorable lesson about character. We were at our local grocery store, and I spotted a candy treat that I wanted. This particular king-size version of the candy was little more than a block of sugar with artificial coloring and flavoring, and my mother wisely refused the purchase. I can still remember the little navy raincoat with the deep pockets that I was wearing. Out of view of my mother, I slipped that king-size childhood delicacy into one of my pockets.

Hours later when hanging up my coat, Mom discovered the candy I had forgotten about in its secret hiding place. She quizzed me as to how I obtained it. I don't remember every detail about the various explanations I tried to offer. I only remember that I lied. At five years old, I was already a thief and a liar! Right then, my mother determined to ensure that these mistakes became teachable moments in my young life.

During our next weekly grocery trip, Mom took me to meet the manager and return the stolen candy. All the way to the store, I was certain I would go to jail. With a quivering lip and watery eyes, I handed the candy to the manager and apologized for my wrongdoing. There were no arrests or visits with police officers. But one thing I am sure of, I never again took something that did not belong to me.

Now, as a mother of three grown children, I realize something else about that memory. For most of my life, I have reflected on that story in terms of how it grew my character. Actually, however, it was a testimony of my mother's character. As hard as it was for me to go back and face that grocery store manager, it was much more difficult for my mother. It would have been easier to take the candy from me, punish me at home, and not admit to anyone what her child had done. As parents, when our children make mistakes, especially when they are young, we often see those mistakes as a reflection of our own parenting.

Thankfully, my mother cared more about my long-term character growth than she did about her temporary embarrassment. She exhibited her integrity and role modeled for me important qualities that would mold my character in the years to come.

That incident early in my childhood helped me secure a "good name" and instill in me the character I would need to be successful in every role in my life. Long before I started school and began to be influenced by others, the foundation of my character was formed. Leadership author, podcaster, and pastor Carey Nieuwhof writes, "Developing your character is never easy, which is why so many people abandon the pursuit. But it's so worth it because you bring who you are to everything you do."[1]

What qualities come to mind when you think of someone of outstanding character? Perhaps you think of a person with a strong sense of purpose and mission. Often, we think of people who have an established set of core values that are demonstrated consistently. The elements of a meaningful purpose, a compelling mission, and demonstrated core values are critical to character formation. A good reputation of admirable character is a great start to getting a job, keeping a job, and growing a career.

Determine Your Personal Purpose

The most important question we will ever ask is *why*: Why am I here? Why do I exist? Why was I created? Asking lots of why questions leads us to our life's calling. Understanding our calling is critical to finding a career that gives our work life meaning. Without a calling, a job is just work. When we find a calling, it engages the core of our being and drives us to fulfill our goals and dreams.

It is from a calling that we find or formulate our personal purpose, discovering our reason for being placed on this planet. Why was I created? What is my unique contribution to this world? One of the most significant roles that leaders in our lives play is helping us find our purpose. Work is only one of the ways we live out our purpose. Generally, a purpose permeates every aspect of our lives and is demonstrated in every connection and role we play.

A personal purpose informs every single major decision we make in life, including career choice and where we choose to work. Ultimately, it is likely to impact other decisions too, such as who our mate will be if we marry, how we serve others, who we worship, how we parent, and what kind of friend we are to the people around us.

Jackie Robinson, the first African American to play major league baseball in the modern era, wrote in his autobiography, "A life is not important except for the impact it has on other lives."[2] It's true. Every other pursuit in life, including fame, wealth, materialism, and popularity, fades the moment our life ends. A life whose purpose is rooted in positive influence and impact is far more likely to be remembered and celebrated.

Develop a Personal Mission

A second element in developing our character is determining our mission. If purpose answers the *why* question, then mission answers the *what* question. What do we want to accomplish during our lifetime? What meaningful goals do we want to set for ourselves and achieve?

Once we discover our personal mission, we are more likely to achieve it by writing it down, measuring our progress, celebrating milestones along the way, and recalibrating when we get off course. Mission statements help keep us focused on the goals we want to achieve in life. Without a clear mission, it is easy to get distracted and chase the means to an end instead of the result we truly desire.

When we understand and articulate our mission, we see that our work is simply one of the means to accomplishing the mission, not the mission itself. Two of my favorite examples of people with clear missions are Oprah Winfrey and Sir Richard Branson.

What do we think of when we think about Oprah Winfrey? A billionaire businesswoman? A talk-show host? A media mogul? A philanthropist? She is all these things, but none of them are listed in her personal mission. These are all means by which she accomplishes her mission: "I wanted to be a teacher. And to be known for inspiring my students to be more than they thought they could be."[3] Every other role she plays is to provide her the opportunity to teach and inspire others.

What about Sir Richard Branson? He has created a reputation as a brand development guru, serial entrepreneur, customer-experience giant, and daring innovator. None of these roles are listed in his mission statement, but they are the means for him to achieve it. His mission: "Have fun in your journey through life and learn from your mistakes."[4] All of those roles contribute to his mission to have fun in life.

Creating and verbalizing a personal mission is important because our mission provides a filter through which to make decisions, including decisions about your career. Starting with the end in mind greatly enhances the probability that you will eventually meet your career and life goals. Dr. Gail Matthews, a psychology professor at Dominican University in California, conducted a study with 270 participants. She learned from the study that you are 42 percent more likely to achieve your goals if you write them down.[5]

Start small with short-term goals and work to refine your goal-setting process to timelines that make sense for your stage in life and career. What works for me is to start the year with annual goals for each part of my life: spiritual, mental, emotional, physical, family, and career. I then take my annual goals and create a monthly plan with measurable interim goals. Finally, on Sunday nights I begin each week by evaluating the previous week against my goals and planning for the next week what I need to do to keep me on track to achieve my monthly goals. Writing them down, either using a digital application or on hard copy, has helped me to easily see where I am and make any needed adjustments to fulfill my goals.

Without an intentional plan to keep you on track to get you where you want to go, it is less likely you will achieve what you intend to accomplish. Such a plan helps us make quick pivots when faced with a crisis or unexpected opportunities too.

Choose Your Personal Core Values

The final characteristic needed to help develop our character is a set of personal core values. These values define the beliefs we hold most dear and articulate them in a way that can be demonstrated by our behavior. For instance, if we believe in the importance of serving others, then service might become a personal core value. We demonstrate this value by the behavior of serving others in our lives and by extending a spirit of service to people we don't even know. Our character becomes known by the behaviors that reflect our deepest beliefs that we articulate as our core values.

Some of our values are engrained in us early in life because we see them communicated and exhibited by the influential people in our lives. Parents, other family members, teachers, coaches, and pastors help us form our values long before we can articulate them. They are formed through stories, lessons, and demonstrated behaviors.

I love a story I read on social media about a mom who used a special moment to teach her child about the core value of generosity. As the story goes, her little one was beginning to ask questions about the existence of Santa Claus. She gently led her son through the discovery that it was now time for him to become a Santa Claus. She explained the very special responsibility of identifying the needs of others, selecting a gift to meet the need, and then giving the gift anonymously.

When it was time for him to identify a person who needed something, he chose a lady who lived on his street. She wasn't particularly kind, and when his ball accidentally landed in her yard, she would not allow him to come inside the fence to retrieve it. Often, she yelled at the children in the neighborhood. On his way to school each day, he watched as she walked outside and down the driveway to retrieve the morning newspaper. He noticed she was barefoot and decided the gift he needed to get her was a new pair of slippers.

To buy slippers, he needed to know what size, so he hid in the bushes one Saturday and discerned that she had a medium-sized foot. The young boy gathered his allowance money, went to the store, and purchased a pair of soft, warm, medium-sized slippers. He carefully wrapped them and added a beautiful Christmas bow and waited for the opportunity to sneak them under her fence without being seen. Finally, one evening right before Christmas, when all the lights in her house were off, he walked down the street and pushed the package under the gate.

A few days later, looking out the window, he saw the woman walking down her driveway, and much to his excitement she was wearing the slippers. From that Christmas on, he was a "Santa Claus." When his brother began to wonder about Santa Claus, he helped with his indoctrination into the secret society.[6]

For many of us, that is exactly how our core values were developed. An influential adult in our life taught us a lesson through a story or experience, and that lesson became part of our belief system. As adults, we have the opportunity to implement them, add to them, or choose our own set of core values.

These values are very important because they represent the core of our being and are a window into our soul. They are crucial elements of our own character and are worthy of careful selection, nurturing, and demonstration. These values represent our moral compass and can be a guide that points to "true north" whenever we become disoriented.

Without a compass to guide us, it is easy to lose our way. Core values are the guideposts on the journey to living out our purpose and achieving our mission. They help form boundaries to keep us from wandering off the trail, and they clearly describe the behaviors that we desire to exhibit.

Character is a result of nature and nurture. We were created with certain personality traits, strengths, and preferences designed within us. During childhood, our character is nurtured by the influences in our lives: parents, other family members, friends, teachers, coaches, employers, community and church leaders, and others who influence us. Even if we have not been positively influenced and nurtured, we can always choose to develop our own character. If you did not grow up with positive influences to help you develop the character needed to be successful, seek them out now. Find a mentor in your community, church, college, or even online through various opportunities on professional sites. Character grounded in a meaningful personal purpose to pursue, a challenging mission to achieve, and core values to demonstrate our deepest beliefs is an excellent start to a successful career.

Don't Give Up When You Don't Know What to Do

Some people grow up knowing exactly what they want to do. For others, it is confusing and frustrating as they try to determine their purpose and mission. Sometimes, circumstances derail us from what we thought would be our life purpose and we have to discover a new one.

From the time my husband, Ashley, was about thirteen, he wanted to be a pastor. As a teen, he prepared himself for the purpose of serving the church. He set goals and pursued the education he would need to eventually lead to ordination as a pastor.

While in college, he served several churches, first as an associate pastor. Then at a small church, he was invited to be the senior pastor. Preaching each week and nurturing his small but older congregation was a dream come true. He was convinced he was living out his purpose and doing the very thing he was made to do.

We married during his senior year of college, and after graduation we returned to our home city of Atlanta. Ashley found an opportunity to be an associate pastor near where we were raised. We were very excited because it meant that we could be near our families. I eventually changed jobs to be closer to the community in which we were serving, and we bought a house nearby. It seemed that we were on our way, and he was achieving his dream of serving others and living out his faith.

A few years into his ministry, circumstances became very difficult, and it was apparent that Ashley needed to make a ministry change. If he stayed in the ministry, I would need to resign my job, and we would have to leave our extended families and serve elsewhere. We decided we wanted to stay in the Atlanta area—meaning I would stay at the Chick-fil-A support center and he would find another calling. It sounded simple, except it wasn't. The only thing he'd ever dreamed of being was a pastor. He would certainly continue to serve the church, but he had to choose a new vocation.

Changing jobs is far easier than finding or changing a calling. Regardless of our age or stage of life, having a purpose to pursue is critical to our own well-being. What do you do when you don't know what you want to do?

First, assess where you are and what your general interests are. While making money is critical to making a living, doing something you enjoy is important too. Think about the interests and activities that bring you the most joy. In finding my own calling, I knew I needed a job that used my writing and communication skills and gave me the opportunity to actively and continuously engage with people. Originally, I thought that path would be through a journalism career, but my skills led me in a very different direction into business. I was still able to pursue those interests but differently than I originally anticipated.

Second, consider your strengths. What do you do better than most people? Of those strengths, which ones can be used on the job? What do other people say you do well? Sometimes we cannot see our own strengths as well as others do, so it is a good idea to ask others to help you identify your strengths.

Next, recognize areas of non-strength. What do you not do so well that you want to avoid in your vocation? What are you not naturally wired to do? Be sure to consider what you don't like to do. Again, trusted advisors are valuable in providing the insight you need.

Also, reflect on what experiences you have had. What did you enjoy the most? Do you like to travel or stay close to home? Do you like working in teams or individually? Are you better in a job that allows you variety, or do you enjoy a more predictable role? Think about your past experiences and evaluate what you enjoyed and the types of experiences you want to avoid.

Lastly, consider what the world needs that you offer. What causes need your help? What vocations value your interests, experiences, and skills? What problems exist that will be solved by someone with your strengths, experiences, and skill set?

Use resources around you to help you assess each of these items and determine a career path. If you are in high school or college, visit with guidance counselors and career counseling staff. They can also refer you to outside resources, such as assessments, courses, and websites, to explore to help you discover your calling and vocation.

It's not unusual at all to find that you don't know what career to pursue or to feel unsure if you need to pursue a new career. My husband thought about the other interests he had in life. Earlier, he was fascinated with flying and aviation. So he decided to pursue a career as an air traffic controller.

It was not an automatic shift for him, and the path was not straight. For a season while he applied to the Federal Aviation Administration Academy and waited to be selected, he relied on past experiences and used the skills he had obtained while working part-time in college. He worked for a men's clothing store to pay his bills while he waited for his next opportunity. Eventually, he was accepted into the program and spent three years in training before achieving his goal of being a journeyman air traffic control specialist.

Many people experience uncertainty when determining what to do as a career, and some even experience it multiple times during a career. Sometimes the change is internally driven, and sometimes there are circumstances beyond our control. During the COVID-19 pandemic, resulting in a skyrocketing unemployment rate, some people had to switch careers and find new vocations due to near elimination of jobs in certain sectors of the workforce.

The most important thing to do in times of career uncertainty is to keep going. Get started in something, and keep searching to find the work you were made to do. If you keep doing the next thing, you will eventually find the right thing.

WHAT'S MY STORY?

1. How has my character been developed?
2. What is my personal purpose? How can I make my purpose more meaningful?
3. What is my personal mission? How am I measuring that mission? Is it time for me to set a new mission that reflects my current season of life?

4. What are my core values? How well am I living out my core values? What behaviors do I need to change to be more reflective of my values?

5. Who positively influenced my character the most in my life? Which traits of that influencer do I want to emulate? Who negatively influenced my character? Which traits do I want to avoid or improve?

2

Cultivating Your Competency

At the young age of ten, I had my first true entrepreneurial venture. A family friend owned a grocery store, and he helped me set up my first business. Each week during the summer, I placed an order with him for candy, snacks, and soft drinks. Our house was on the path to the neighborhood swimming pool, and each morning and afternoon, I set up my own little shop on our back patio. In the morning, my friends and the neighborhood locals would stop by and purchase their snacks from me. My prices were the same as the grocery store and better than the vending machine at the pool. In the afternoon, the hungry swimmers, unable to wait until dinnertime, would pass by again on the way home and stop in to pick up their snack stash.

This endeavor worked out quite well for me. I purchased the goods at wholesale prices, sold them for retail prices, and used the profits to buy stock for the next week. Beyond earning spending money, I learned a lot about how to work. This little summer business taught me to be dependable. If I did not open when my customers expected me to open, they would soon stop showing up to buy my merchandise. I learned how to plan inventory, keep the books, and deliver the basics of good customer service. By preparing flyers about my business and distributing them throughout the neighborhood, I learned marketing skills.

Many of us learned how to work in similar ways. Before we were old enough to be hired by a business, we babysat, mowed lawns, cleaned pools, and sold everything from lemonade to wrapping paper. As you are preparing to get a job and start a career, don't discount what those early jobs taught you. Value early employment, volunteer work, and even fundraising efforts, and don't be afraid to talk about them as part of your experience. Employers are curious about the work ethic of future employees, and sharing with them how you developed early competency can be a strong conversation starter.

Bob Iger, former CEO of the Walt Disney Company, talks about the importance of early jobs: "I started working in eighth grade, shoveling snow and babysitting and working as a stock boy in a hardware store. At fifteen, I got a job as the summer janitor in my school district. It involved cleaning every heater in every classroom, then moving on to the bottom of every desk, making sure they were gum-free when the school year started. Cleaning gum from the bottoms of a thousand desks can build character, or at least a tolerance for monotony, or something."[1]

These and other early part-time jobs give us valuable experience in being accountable to others, help us network for career jobs, and can be instrumental in helping pay for advanced education. Recognize the importance of early job skills and the value of learning accountability.

When our third son was ten, he too started his own business. He was quite industrious and always looking for something to do and ways to earn money. It all started with baseball cards. Trey bought the large boxes for eight to ten dollars and searched through them to find the valuable cards in the bunch. He then sold the valuable cards for their worth online. He quickly learned that he was not Amazon and not to advertise free shipping. One customer from Puerto Rico bought a very valuable card, but the shipping cost my son his entire profit and then some.

We begin learning competency to work very early in life. Education, training, and experiences from childhood and young adulthood combine to prepare us for the world of work. We can learn not only leadership skills in these early experiences but how to be good followers as well. Accountability to a teacher, coach, piano teacher, band director, and boss helps prepare a young person for an eventual career.

Years ago, before my children were old enough to work, I began a private file of lessons I wanted to be sure to share with them when they began to consider their first jobs. It was full of both best practices from great job candidates and mistakes of job candidates. Leading human resources for a multibillion-dollar company gave me a lot of material, which of course remained confidential even though I used the individual situations as teachable moments.

Most of the lessons learned from the candidates were character driven. The candidate who remembered to write a handwritten note not only to me but also to each person he met in the process represented the highest level of courtesy and respect. The person who lied about her grade point average or treated the receptionist poorly was a reminder of behavior to avoid. These behaviors either accelerated the process for a candidate or became a barrier to receiving a job offer.

Based on these experiences, following are some important reminders for preparing for early work opportunities or first jobs:

- *Don't just choose a job.* Choose a person for whom you really desire to work. You are choosing to associate yourself with a company and its people—be sure it is a match to you. This is the place where your résumé begins. Are you proud of the product or service?

- *Apply, apply, apply.* For a first job, you may have to apply for many jobs just to land one interview. If it is a place you really desire to work and you are turned down, apply again. It's not unusual to submit ten to fifteen applications to get one interview. Persistence can be an attractive quality to a potential employer.

- *Prepare for the interview.* If you have no work experience, be prepared to talk about any responsibility you have assumed in the past. Highlight volunteer work, babysitting, lawn mowing, and even lemonade-stand experience. Share any experience you have had fundraising for school or community projects as well. You will want to highlight anything that demonstrates your initiative and drive. Be sure that you talk about not only what you did but also why you did it. Your potential employer may be interested to know what motivates you.

- *Be yourself.* During the interview, answer questions in a way that helps the potential employer get to know you. Prepare for the talking points you want to communicate during the interview, and use opportunities to share those as questions are asked. Practice with someone else before the interview so you can get comfortable answering the questions. Always end the interview by thanking the interviewer and asking when you should expect to hear about next steps.

- *Get experience and experiment.* You might have to do a few or many things you don't want to do. The first job one of my sons had was cleaning swimming pools. While he certainly learned a lot about cleaning and maintaining pools, he also learned a lot of life lessons from his manager. His manager saw my son's potential but could also see that he needed some direction. During his lunch break, my son went through the drive-thru of his favorite restaurant; his manager brown-bagged it, explaining that he could not afford to eat lunch at a restaurant every day. On one occasion, his manager asked him if I was able to take earned vacation time anytime I choose. When my son replied affirmatively, he encouraged him by saying, "Get a job like that." Sometimes, experience is found in the lessons we learn along the way, not in the work itself.

- *Be grateful to someone who will give you a chance.* Hiring someone with no experience is a big risk. Not only does that company have to teach you the job, sometimes they also have to teach you how to work. You make it much easier for them when you show up on time or early, dressed appropriately and ready to work. That not only helps you keep your job, but it also allows your new boss to focus on developing you in your job rather than wondering if you will work out at all.

- *Think forward.* Recognize that every day of your first job is a stepping-stone to the rest of your career. Grow relationships. Do more than is asked. Be positive, and learn something new every day.

Part-time jobs early in life contribute to understanding ourselves and the unique gifts, talents, and skill sets we have to offer. They are important experiences to pursuing a career and finding success in our work. Early employment can be important preparation for learning how to find a job, keep a job, and grow a career.

WHAT'S MY STORY?

1. What are some of my early experiences that have helped me build competency for my career?
2. How will I characterize those experiences to add value to my future career job interviews?
3. What specific skills did I gain from those early experiences?

3

Finding a Job

Pursuing a career is much more difficult than getting a job. It's a longer-term commitment, and the choice we make can impact our overall happiness. The main purpose of early part-time and odd jobs discussed in the previous chapter is to gain some very basic work experience. Those early jobs teach us how to respond to directions and meet and exceed expectations. We learn the basics of arriving on time, staying on task, and following directions. These experiences better prepare us to pursue the first job of our career choice.

The first job in our chosen career is a stepping-stone to the next forty or more years of our work lives. Additionally, we will average forty or more hours per week in a job that is incredibly important not only for the future but also for our current day-to-day livelihood. The first career job is a critical choice and requires tremendous intentionality to find the right fit to launch our career.

Securing the first or a new career position takes a lot of preparation. Finding the right organization to join, applying for jobs, interviewing, providing solid references, and following up with hiring managers for multiple opportunities necessitate time, diligence, and patience. When the market is good, jobs are plentiful, but finding the right role is more tedious. Sorting through various opportunities and selecting the one that best fits our skills and experience is critical to keeping our career moving in the direction that meets our long-term goals. In a tight job market, our ability to differentiate ourselves and be competitive among multiple candidates becomes even more important.

Develop an Online Résumé

In a vast majority of cases, in the early stages of the recruiting process, companies use job recruiting sites, such as LinkedIn and Indeed, to identify potential candidates. In fact, 87 percent of recruiters report that they use LinkedIn to vet candidates before ever looking at any résumés.[1] It's still a good idea to prepare a physical paper copy of your résumé for organizations that request one, but most requests will be for online completion of an expression of interest form or digital application.

Employers use technology to scan online profiles and digital résumés for key words that match the skills they are seeking for a role. Ensure that your résumé highlights the key skills the employer is seeking. Load your online profiles and your résumé with descriptions of your acquired skills that match the job profile. If you have a lot of experience or a deep skill set, create different versions of your résumé that highlight your relevant skills and experience for each role you pursue. The recruiting website Indeed includes many available online assessments to immediately inform employers of your capabilities.

Once you have outlined your skills, the next focus area is your experience. Start with your most recent relevant experience and then add previous relevant experiences. If you have not yet obtained experience in your chosen career field, then simply start with your most recent experience and include where you have worked. In this case, it might serve you best to begin your résumé with other credentials that match the job, such as education or acquired skills and certifications.

While some of your previous roles may not seem pertinent, try not to arrange experiences in such a way that it leaves gaps in employment. If you have a consistent track record of employment, demonstrate it in the résumé. If there are gaps, be prepared to explain those in the interview.

When you describe your experiences, be sure to use data to emphasize the results you achieve rather than only stating your responsibilities. Employers want to know the results you have achieved more than what tasks you have completed. Data includes the measurements used to define success in the role and a description of your performance against those measurements. For instance, if you are a sales professional, talk about the total number of new clients and revenue you brought to the organization. If you are a computer programmer, describe the solutions you designed to solve problems or challenges in the organization.

Unless specifically asked in an online profile, you may want to avoid stating your objective. This could limit an employer's interest if the available position does not match your stated objective. Instead, use the space for a career summary that gives an overview of all your skills and experiences.

The look of your résumé is important too. Be sure it is clean, concise, and on one page. The résumé is intended to be a quick overview to spark a recruiter's interest, not a review of your entire career. Your résumé will likely be scanned in just a few seconds, so leave off fancy graphics and layouts and try to draw the prospective employer right to the highlights of your skills, experiences, and interests.

This may sound obvious, but be sure that everything you put on a résumé or post to an online profile is true. It is very easy and inexpensive to fact-check a candidate's information, and any inaccuracies will likely eliminate you from consideration. Years ago, I used grade point averages as criteria for certain entry-level positions in the company. These thresholds were set by the hiring managers for the specific roles requiring a high level of proficiency and knowledge. Mainly, they were used to evaluate candidates for highly technical jobs and candidates who lacked job experience. However, I learned it was also an easy test for honesty or detail orientation.

At that time, college transcripts were available for two dollars each. On the application, candidates were informed that a transcript would be requested, and they were asked to provide their college GPAs. It was an automatic part of the process to request the transcript for any candidate the company chose to pursue beyond an initial interview. It was astounding to see how many people limited their future by not carefully providing an accurate GPA. Rarely were candidates turned down because their GPA was too low, but they were usually turned down for significant discrepancies in what they reported and what the college or university provided to us.

When we received notification of a discrepancy and the difference was minor, I did not address it. But when it was significant, I always gave the candidate an opportunity to explain. The discrepancy was usually for one of two reasons: either the candidate was intentionally dishonest or the candidate was not detail-oriented enough to confirm the accuracy of the requested information. Either reason was an indication to pass on the candidate for the role. Be sure that all the information you place on your résumé or application or state in an interview is true.

Online recruiting platforms have made preparing a résumé much quicker and easier. It's a great place to start your job search. In fact, it's a good idea to keep an updated profile on all the major online platforms. Be sure to attach your résumé to online profiles.

Following are some suggested steps to maximize your online presence on recruiting sites; they are similar to the way you manage your résumé:

- *Keep your profile up-to-date.* Every time you acquire a new skill, gain a new experience, or obtain additional education, be sure to take a moment and update your profile.
- *Refresh your headline from time to time.* When recruiters are searching for candidates, they get a quick snapshot of you

from your headline. If you are in a job search, this is the place to be concise and clear about the role you are seeking and your career objective. "Experienced social media guru pursuing opportunity to support start-up entrepreneurs" is an example of an effective headline. You have a few seconds to stand out among the rest as recruiters scan the feed.

- *Use these sites to network.* Networking leads to interviewing opportunities. Online recruiting platforms expedite networking. Search the site for people from your college or university who work for the company with whom you want to interview. Connect with them and ask questions about the role and the organization. If you know them well, ask for a recommendation. Join the professional groups included on the platform to find out about job opportunities. Attend the events sponsored by the platform to meet people in person. Remember that the quality of your networking is more important than the quantity. Go deep in building relationships with people in your network, even at the expense of establishing fewer connections.

- *Include all of your skills on your profile.* Experts suggest that hard-copy résumés be one page in length. Online profiles do not have the same size limitations, so be sure to share all of your relevant skills, certifications, and capabilities in your profile.

- *Focus on your most recent experience.* If this is your first career role but you previously have had part-time jobs and internships, highlight the ones in which you can most easily describe your contributions and what you learned from the experience. If you have had multiple jobs, expand on the current or most recent job and reduce the content from earlier jobs.

- *Quantify experiences on the profile as you do on your résumé.* For example, if in a former job you were responsible for analyzing customer data, quantify the number of reports you reviewed and how many customers were represented in the data.

- *Check spelling, grammar, and punctuation.* Make sure your online presence is as professional looking as a hard-copy résumé.

Following these steps can help you land the interview you desire with an organization that meets your career objectives. When the recruiter selects your résumé or profile as someone to pursue, make sure you are ready. I have seen people derail themselves by not preparing for contact by the recruiter. You are likely to receive a phone call, a text, or an email. Be sure your voice-mail message is professional. I called a candidate one time and heard a rap music introduction followed by "Yo! You know what to do, so do it at the beep." That's great for planning to hang out with friends, but not so great when expecting to hear from a recruiter.

If you have auto responses set up in email, be sure they represent you as a serious job candidate. Choose a professional email address related to your name. Save the cute ones for spammers and sign ups to mailing lists.

Manage Social Media in Your Job Search

Bart was thirty days into his new job search when he discovered the company that best matched his interests, background, and experience. Now, it was time for him to help them discover him. During a time of high unemployment and high competition for jobs, Bart had to be very intentional about getting the attention of recruiters. How did Bart create a presence with his targeted company among the many candidates vying for the position? He became their biggest "super fan" on social media.

Becoming a super fan is more than liking, commenting, and sharing and takes some skill to do well. Bart incorporated a few key tips into his social media activities, and he became known by the company. Later, he also received a job offer.

What did Bart do to create a candidate brand to a potential employer without becoming a social media pest? The following steps might help you get noticed by the company of your dreams too:

- *Update all your social media accounts before you begin using social media for your job search.* Be sure they are representative of the personal brand you want to project to potential employers. Your personal brand is how you represent yourself. It is the unique combination of capabilities, experiences, and personal values that you want others to know about you. This means an updated, professional headshot, a headline in the profile that clearly states your objective, and removal of any posts or comments that are not true to your personal brand.
- *Follow the company, its key leaders, and people who are involved in selecting talent on professional social media platforms.* Don't send invitations to become Facebook friends or follow their personal accounts on Instagram. You can become friends and snap chat after you land the job. Stick to the professional pages and accounts associated with the company.
- *Comment, like, and share on the social media platforms you are following no more often than daily.* Try to comment two to three times each week minimally. Make the content meaningful. Don't post short answers, such as "Yes, I agree!" Instead, add value to your content by expressing an opinion that reveals the depth of your experience. When you share the company's content, don't just push the share button. Add a comment as to the value of the content, and use it as an opportunity to share your own expertise. Did a company leader write a book? Read it and post a review on LinkedIn.

Did they win an award or receive recognition? Share the post and tag the people you know from the interviewing process in your post.

- *Don't be just a social media fan but a real fan.* Learn everything you can about the company from their social media sites, and use what is posted to promote your love of their brand. When you receive an invitation to interview, you will already be well prepared to talk about your knowledge of the organization. Employers want to know that you have done your homework.

- *Remember that not everything on social media is true.* Be discerning about what you choose to comment on and share. It really goes without saying, but don't share derogatory posts about the company or anyone else either. Share only what is positive, and you will quickly become a super fan.

- *Plan to post on social media at a time when you are most likely to be noticed.* Monday morning is usually a very busy time for most business leaders. However, since LinkedIn is a professional site, it is used during working hours. Target 10:00 a.m. to 12:00 p.m. Tuesday through Thursday for best results. Facebook and Instagram posts are noticed later in the day, so save them for after work hours. Twitter and Pinterest are fairly active twenty-four hours a day, but the people whose attention you are trying to attract are sleeping in the middle of the night and might wonder why you are not if you are posting at 3:00 a.m. Also, employers want fully engaged employees, so if you currently have a job, you don't want your potential employer to see you spending hours on social media on the clock of your present employer.

- *Social media posts and even private messages are more likely to be seen than email.* If you are looking for a way to get the attention of a company's recruiter, use private messaging on social media platforms. They get hundreds if not thousands of emails each day in their work email inbox. Private messages are generally fewer and spread across platforms. Of course, some companies have policies against responding in private messaging altogether, but at least your name will pop up in their inbox.

- *Create content so engaging that the company wants to follow you.* Add images or video to every post. If you are posting a quote, put it in a format that helps it stand out, such as within an image or with a graphic. Take a poll or ask a question to capture attention. Remember, consistency is the key. If you want to be noticed, then connect every day.

- *If you are not selected for the first role, don't give up and stop social media activity.* Keep up the engagement and add other companies into the mix that also interest you. The timing might not be right for your dream company, but another opportunity may come along with another company that you find you love just as much. Once you have invested in a strong candidate brand and social media presence, don't abandon the effort. Instead, keep it active.

When Bart started his job search, he had not applied for a new job in ten years. During his last job change, social media was not as sophisticated or in use as much as it is today. However, in following these steps, he quickly went from novice to skilled and was able to attract the attention of the recruiters for the job he desired. He set himself apart from the other applicants, and the recruiters took notice.

Prepare for the Interview

After preparing your résumé and creating a stellar online presence, you are ready to respond to recruiters about potential opportunities. You would not go onstage for a performance or play in a big game without practicing. When it comes to your career, practicing for interviews is just as important and a crucial part of interview preparation. Ask a friend or family member to conduct a mock interview with you. Don't just practice in person, but also conduct mock interviews virtually, so you can be sure you have prepared for that scenario as well.

Mental preparation for an interview includes knowing yourself, knowing your audience, looking the part, developing thoughtful questions, and securing references ahead of the interview.

The Online Video Interview

Often, the first interview is virtual and requires an application such as Skype or Zoom. Many of us now work remotely, and we are quite comfortable with these applications. However, when it comes to an interview, be sure to know exactly how to log on with the correct link well ahead of the scheduled time of the interview. Use headphones or earbuds with a built-in or external microphone to ensure that you and the interviewer can clearly hear each other. Computer microphones and speakers can sometimes make that difficult. Test your Wi-Fi connection, and select a private location free of external noise and interruption for the interview. Ensure that your web camera is operating correctly, and test your sound before the interview begins.

Dress the same for a virtual interview as you would for interviewing in person. While these interviews mean that you will likely be on camera only from the shoulders up, go ahead and dress the part completely. You will feel more in the role of an interview and avoid any unexpected camera shots. Prints and patterns sometimes cause distortion with video, so you may want to steer clear of them and opt for bright solids instead. Lastly, be sure to conduct the interview in an area with good lighting. Invest in a clip-on ring light for your device to improve the lighting. Poor lighting will provide only a shadow of you and make you look as though you are in a witness protection program.

A few years ago, my middle son had an important interview with the CEO of a technology firm with which he was pursuing a position. This was before the COVID-19 pandemic, and virtual meetings were not the norm. Trevor was young in his career, and while he had used Skype, he had not used other online meeting applications. The recruiter who scheduled the interview had not provided the link for it. My son rushed home from his current job to log in and start his interview only to find that he did not have the right application downloaded. His interview began awkwardly with him having to admit he had not used the application before and needed time to download it. Always give yourself extra time when technology is involved in your interview. Fortunately, his then-future boss saw greater potential in him and offered him a job, which he accepted.

If the online interview goes well, it is likely the candidate will be invited for an in-person interview.

The In-Person Interview

Sarah had been out of the job market for over ten years, raising her family. College tuition expenses for her children made it necessary for her to return to her career. While she was excited about a new chapter, extra income, and developing new relationships, she was also understandably nervous about interviewing. It had been two decades since she interviewed for a job, and she was unsure not only how to dress for business casual but also how to talk about her experience as a stay-at-home parent.

Sarah's situation is not unusual. What to wear is easily solved by a quick check on the company's website and advice from the recruiter. However, determining how to answer interview questions takes a little more thought. Careful research of the company, the person with whom she will interview, and others who are employed there will prepare her for the big day.

When Sarah came to see me, I gave her the following tips to ace the interview:

- *Research the organization.* You cannot learn too much about the company and the person conducting the interview. Social media sites make it especially easy to find almost anything you need to know. Learn the primary products, services, and customers of the organization. Determine the culture by knowing the purpose, mission, and core values. Review the background of the interviewer to prepare for potential interview questions and aid in casual conversation.

- *Know where the interview is located, and be on time.* Determine the time you need to leave home or the hotel if it is an out-of-town interview. If you are driving yourself, allow enough time to find the location, navigate traffic, and locate parking. Be sure to ask the interview scheduler where to park. If you plan to use public transportation, be sure you know the routes and schedules and give yourself extra time for delays. Plan to arrive at least fifteen minutes early. You can never be too early, but being late could impact your candidacy. Some candidates do a practice run to the location the day before to be sure they know exactly where they are going.

- *Know yourself.* Spend time creating a strong profile of who you are, your experience, your skills, and what you know. This is more than preparing your résumé, which you obviously need. This is examining who you are and what contributions you can bring to an organization. Your work experience might be dated, but your life experience is not. Be prepared to talk about what your current season of life is teaching you and the skills you have obtained.

- *Look the part.* Before words ever come out of your mouth, you will need to look the part of the role you wish to land. In today's business-casual work environment, this can be tricky.

You want to be neither underdressed nor overdressed, but it is always better to err on the side of the latter. Search for photos of the workplace on the company's website, Glassdoor, Indeed, LinkedIn, or other social media sites. This will give you your first visual cue.

Also, ask the recruiter who invited you for the interview about the organization's dress code. Then dress a little nicer than what is standard for the company. If you have the resources, invest in a new outfit. If not, then wear something you feel great in that is neatly pressed and give your shoes a quick shine. A fresh hair style, neatly manicured nails, a well-trimmed beard, and conservative jewelry and makeup help make a strong first impression. Throughout the interviewing process, you will learn more about the appearance requirements of the organization and can decide if it feels comfortable to you.

- *Greet the interviewer with a smile and direct eye contact.* This tip might be considered obvious, but when candidates are nervous, they sometimes forget to do this, and it's important for setting the tone of the interview. These two behaviors signal to the interviewer that you have healthy confidence in yourself. Smiling and making eye contact also make the interviewer comfortable with you right from the start. The more comfortable the interviewer, the better the interview will go.

- *Answer the questions thoroughly, truthfully, and transparently but don't ramble.* You will have anticipated some of the questions you are likely to be asked, and you will have thought about your answers. Those will be easy. If you are asked an unexpected question, take a few seconds to gather your thoughts before answering and then do so as completely as possible. It is not necessary to explain everything you know about a subject. Hit the highlights, and give the interviewer the opportunity to ask follow-up questions to obtain further information. Most initial interviews are scheduled for thirty to forty-five minutes. If you ramble too long on the first few questions, the interviewer will not be able to learn everything needed to decide whether you are the right candidate. Practicing with a friend or family member will help you create a focused narrative about your experience.

- *Continue to smile and breathe.* Yes, really. People forget to breathe, and it makes a negative impression on the interviewer and can cause you to have brain fog in the interview. Be sure to pause between your sentences, and take the cue from the interviewer on whether you need to say more. If you pause, breathe, and smile and the interviewer does not start talking, then elaborate on your response. This is the interviewer's cue that you should continue.

- *Select thoughtful questions to ask the interviewer.* A common mistake that candidates make is to ask the interviewer a question easily found on the company website. Study the website and identify questions you want to ask. Keep questions in an initial interview focused on the company, the specific role you are pursuing, and the team with whom you would be working. Write down your questions so they will be handy when the interviewer offers the opportunity to ask them.

People often ask me, especially those new to the workforce, what type of questions they should ask during an interview. Consider these suggestions:

- How do employees live out the purpose of the organization?
- How is success defined for this role?
- What traits help someone to be successful in this organization's culture?
- How would you describe the performance-feedback process?
- How does the organization support development for employees?

- Why are you interested in me for this role? What do you think I can contribute immediately?
- What goals does the organization hope to achieve this year? In five years? In ten years?
- What is the most important aspect of the organization's culture?
- How is teamwork and collaboration encouraged and achieved?
- What is the turnover rate, and why do people leave this organization?
- What do customers expect from the organization? How much interaction will I have with customers?
- What is the most challenging part of working here?
- How do leaders in this company help strengthen the culture?
- What is a typical day like in this role?
- Has anyone been unsuccessful in this role? Why were they unsuccessful? What could they have done differently to avoid failure?
- How does the organization demonstrate its commitment to innovation? Can you give some examples?
- What process does the company use to listen to employees and incorporate their ideas?
- What are the criteria for advancement from this role?
- What have been the most significant changes to the organization in the last three years?
- What have I not asked that I should ask about the organization?

- *Extend a sincere and warm farewell.* When the interview ends, thank the interviewer for the opportunity and ask when you can expect to hear about next steps and whether to expect a phone call or an email. Obtain business cards or electronic contacts from each person involved in your interview, including the scheduler and the receptionist who greeted you. Send an email follow-up that day to each of them, and specifically mention how that person made your interview special. Send a handwritten note to your interviewer immediately following the interview. Sure, it might end up in the trash or scanned into your electronic candidate file, but few people today send handwritten notes, and it will help you stand out among other candidates.

In addition to these actions, here is a bonus tip: treat every single person you meet, from the receptionist—or scheduler, if the process is completely virtual—to casual introductions to the interviewer, as if they are a part of the selection process. If your actions are inconsistent, that information will likely be conveyed to the decision maker. Many times after an interview, I talked to the receptionist or the driver who transported the candidate to and from the airport. I asked them about their experiences with the candidate. Oftentimes, I received important input from these sources in making a decision. Never assume that anyone with whom you interact is not part of the selection process.

Sarah used the tips I gave her to inform her actions and aced the interview. She landed the job of her dreams for this season of her life and is happily employed, growing her career and making tuition payments for her son and daughter. You too can use these suggestions to ace an interview, land your first-career, mid-career, or second-career job, and begin the next steps of growing your career.

Secure Strong References

Though extremely important, interviewing is just one part of the overall selection process. Another important part is providing references to the potential employer. Often, the recruiter will narrow your list of requested references based on your application, résumé, or online profile. Occasionally, you will be able to choose the references yourself.

Who makes a great reference? Choose an individual to whom you have been accountable during your adult or young-adult life. For candidates who already have work experience, the recruiter will expect to see former employers as references. The company will prefer to speak to someone who supervised you, not the person assigned to employment verifications. Be sure to contact former supervisors and secure their permission before submitting their names as references.

For candidates with very little work experience, select references who are not family members but who know you well and can speak to your character, competency, and chemistry. They might be college professors, coaches, or leaders of volunteer organizations. Even before starting your career, nurture these types of relationships so that they will be available to you when you start applying for jobs. If you network well and maintain the relationships, they will likely be eager to help you start your career. Be sure to ask these individuals for permission to use them as references as well. You don't want them to be surprised by a call or an email from a potential employer. Prepare your list prior to your first interview with name, relationship to you, phone number, and email address.

When you apply for a specific job, talk to your references about the role and why you think it will be a good fit for your skills and experiences. This will help the reference to better answer questions when asked.

Understand the Employer's Point of View

In approaching the interview process, it is important to understand what the hiring manager and the organization are looking for in new employees. In addition to searching online and learning about the company, seek out people you know who either currently work for the company or have worked there in the past. Ask your sources what to expect in the interview and what important qualities a successful candidate will possess. I have repeatedly seen candidates excel at this type of networking and boost their opportunities.

Strong Character

Most employers look for people with strong character. They want to select talent whose character matches the organization. Some of the qualities I use to evaluate character are as follows:

- *A heart for service.* I look for people who are willing to go above and beyond expectations for customers and their fellow teammates. I recognize a heart for service through understanding how a candidate serves others at work, at school, or in the community. I ask for specific examples of service behavior.

- *A sense of personal purpose.* I look for candidates who know who they are and why they are here. They have established a purpose for their career and their life. Candidates with a purpose are able to articulate the purpose in the interview and give examples of how they are living it out day-to-day.

- *An ability to be a team player.* I love personal ambition, but I love ambition for a team's success even more. Team players are known by their support of others and can provide examples of how they contributed to achieving a team's goal.

- *A set of personal core values.* I want to know what a candidate's core values are, how they were developed, and how the candidate demonstrates those values in daily life (see chap. 1). This is more than just a list of character traits. These are the beliefs a candidate holds most dear and uses as a filter to make every decision in life. Review your core values, and be prepared to discuss them.

Competency

All employers look for competency. The following are some of the competency traits I seek:

- *Lifelong learners.* How does the candidate further their abilities and develop additional skills? I may ask what podcasts they listen to, what books they have read, what online courses they have taken.
- *Role-specific skills.* Every role requires a specific skill set. How do I find the candidate who best executes the needed skills? I look for evidence of that ability through interviews, assessments, and references. The candidate's performance in any previous role will also be a strong indicator of potential success in the new role.
- *Clear communication.* Can the candidate explain his work, goals, and passions, in both verbal and written communications? The ability to communicate clearly is critical for almost any role in an organization. The application, online profile, résumé, and follow-up emails all give visual cues for written communication. Verbal communication skills are identified in the video and in-person interviews. Be sure to triple-check all written communication for errors, and practice interview answers to improve verbal communication skills.

Chemistry

All employers look for chemistry that matches the team. There are several indicators I look for to ensure chemistry with the team:

- *Collaboration.* Is the candidate able to collaborate with a team to help achieve team goals and willing to place team goals above personal goals?
- *Fit.* Does the candidate get along well with others? At the same time, is the candidate skilled in offering a diverse point of view?

- *Approachability.* Will clients and others outside of the team find the candidate approachable and enjoyable to work with?
- *Resiliency and agility.* When marketplace conditions suddenly shift, will the candidate be able to quickly adjust to a different role on the team?

When it comes to chemistry, the candidate that impresses me most is someone who can offer a diverse point of view, and yet collaborate in such a way as to have significant influence on others.

Sometimes I am asked which of the three criteria employers look for is most important. They are all important, but character comes first. I can teach someone to do a lot of things, but skill without character can quickly become a liability. But character without competency can create an organization of nice but unskilled people. Competency without chemistry can generate many experts with their own agendas and little regard for the success of the team and the organization. The best candidates are a match in all three of these areas.

Interview Your Future Boss

The decision to work for an organization belongs to you as much as to the organization. They are making a choice about who they want to select, but you have a choice as well. Before your interviewing process concludes, be sure to interview your future boss to make sure that person possesses the character, competency, and chemistry to be a good leader for you. It is likely that you will change bosses often in an organization, but getting off to a good start and setting a path for your future often depends on the person who brings you into the organization.

Consider making some observations about a potential boss during the interview. What attributes in good leaders will help make you successful?

- *Supervisors demonstrate respect and value your experiences.* A supportive manager is going to communicate to you. Generation Z expert Ryan Jenkins suggests that leaders who support you do so with words and an attitude that communicates "I recognize your good work. I value you. We're going places together."[2] Leaders vested in you who are excited to have you on the team will communicate what they think you will bring to the team.

- *Leaders articulate their purpose, mission, and values to you.* They will give examples of how they are leading the team to achieve goals bigger than themselves. Their energy, passion, and motivation will be evident.

- *Managers envision a future path for you, even if it's vague.* If they don't have an idea of what might be next for you, they are not very vested in you. A leader committed to helping you grow your career will communicate the possibilities.

- *Bosses share available developmental opportunities for you.* They are already thinking about how to help you create a self-development plan and what it might include. Organizations committed to developing their staff will be the best places to grow a career.

A positive relationship with a future boss begins during the interviewing process. Just as you are at your best during an interview, your potential boss likely is too. If the individual interviewing you keeps you waiting, appears distracted, seems hurried, and doesn't listen well, it is likely that will be your employment experience with that person as well.

One of my sons was recruited to two companies at the same time and interviewed for both jobs. The one he accepted was with the smaller company. When I asked him why he chose it, he replied that the CEO made him feel like he was not just one of many candidates. Instead, he took time with my son and made him feel as if he was the only candidate. The CEO shared the culture and vision of the company with him and was patient to answer all of my son's questions. After he accepted the job, the CEO continued to behave in the same way, treating him with respect as a valued member of the team.

Inquire about Next Steps

After each interview during the selection process, ask the interviewer when you can expect to be contacted about next steps. If you don't hear back from the company when expected, call or email them. If the company does not give you a follow-up date, contact them one week after your interview. When waiting for a follow-up response, give the company twenty-four hours to call or email. In a tight job market, most companies that have a strong talent-acquisition function are quick to respond to candidates. However, if they don't respond to you, don't give up. Sometimes you must be persistent in order to receive communication about next steps, a job offer, or even an unanticipated no. Every candidate who invests time in applying to an organization and interviewing deserves a response. Don't be shy about asking for one.

The balance is keeping your candidacy visible while not being a pest. I stayed at the second company for which I worked for thirty-three years, but it took a tremendous amount of persistence to initially land a job there. I applied twice and was turned down by a letter both times. After applying the third time, I continued to call once every few weeks for six months before I was invited in for an interview. I heard there was a job opening in advertising, which was the area where I wanted to work. When I learned of an opening in that function, I reached out immediately. Calling at the specific time they had an opening matching my interests significantly increased my odds of being selected.

Now years later, I think a multipronged approach works best when waiting for a reply. Send an email, make a phone call, ping on LinkedIn, send a text, and lastly, as I have said before, really stand out with a handwritten note. Don't necessarily use every channel each day, but mix them up to get your recruiter's attention. Talent-acquisition departments are notoriously understaffed for the volume of work they carry, and they are managing dozens of positions, hundreds of candidates, and several hiring managers. You'll need a strategy for ensuring you receive a timely response.

Hopefully, you will receive a response with the job offer of your dreams and find this advice unnecessary. Should you find yourself in the same situation I was in, don't give up. Politely and persistently continue to follow up. It is highly likely that if you manage the situation professionally, you will develop a relationship with the recruiter that will be helpful in receiving a job offer from either that company or somewhere else.

One young man I know was pursuing a summer internship at a company where one of the senior officers had shown an interest in having him pursue the opportunity. He had talked to the leader several times before the application was even available online. When the job was posted, he applied immediately. I asked him whether he had dropped an email to the senior officer to let him know that he had applied for the job. He said no because he did not want to continue to pester him. I explained to him that this type of networking is important to being selected and that he needed to let the leader know the application had been submitted.

If you have networked within the organization, keep those people apprised of your progress. It will make it much easier for them to advocate for you.

Consider the Job Offer

Congratulations on landing your dream job! Now it's time to consider the offer and make a decision. As a hiring manager and a human resources leader, my goal was to be sure that the candidate was ready to accept the job before I made an offer. That meant I needed to be sure that the salary and benefits met the expectations of the candidate. I needed to consider if a relocation package was part of the offer. Failure on my part to be sure of those expectations could mean disaster in attracting and selecting the best candidate. Hopefully, you have made your intentions and expectations clear, and the offer you receive is reflective of those expectations.

Should you, for some reason, decide not to accept the offer, *do so by telephone and not by email.* That may be counter to today's culture, but you want to be sure you maintain the relationships you have developed during the process. You never know where or how your path may cross with those people in the future. Take the time to at least attempt a call to the hiring manager. Express gratitude for the time invested in you, and explain why you are unable to accept the offer. Also, follow up with a written note to the hiring manager and the recruiter, thanking them for offering you the job and the time they invested in pursuing you.

If you have decided to accept the offer, *be sure you have the offer in writing.* If you are currently employed, you do not want to resign from your current job without a firm written offer in hand. When negotiating a start date with your future employer, be sure to include a two-week notice to your current employer and any time off you wish to take between jobs.

Always offer a two-week notice when leaving a job. Some employers will wish you well (or not) and allow you to leave as soon as you resign. Some will ask you to remain for the two weeks to accommodate a smooth transition within the organization. Not giving or refusing to give a two-week notice is considered unprofessional and might cast you in a bad light should you need a reference from the company in the future. It's also not recommended that you work much longer than two weeks, even if your current employer desires it. Once you have accepted your new job, it is human nature to begin focusing on where you are headed rather than where you are currently.

Before you accept the job offer, be sure your future employer understands your plans to give your current employer a two-week notice. Nearly every company is understanding of this professional practice; if they are not, they might not be the right company for you.

It's been a long process, but you have made it! You now begin a new job and maybe a whole new career. Your next task is to learn how to keep a job.

WHAT'S MY STORY?

1. What updates do I need to make to my online job profiles before applying for jobs?

2. What changes do I need to make to my social media profiles before applying for jobs?

3. Who can help me practice answering interview questions?

4. What income expectations do I have? What benefits are nonnegotiable in a job opportunity?

5. Do I need to update my contact apps for easier follow-up with potential employers? What system should I use to track my job-search process?

KEEP A JOB

PART II

Once you have launched your career and found a job that puts you on track to achieve your goals, focus on how to keep the job and grow your career. According to one study, people who entered the workforce in 2020 will change careers five to seven times and change jobs about every three years.[1]

For these reasons alone, it is incredibly important to maximize every role to ensure it equips you for the next job that will grow your career or prepare you for your next one. Of course, you want to be successful and ensure that when you decide to leave your job, it is on your terms.

Getting off to a good start, building relationships, earning trust with your boss and others, taking good care of yourself, and managing your own performance are important skills and capabilities that will help you keep your job. However, don't get too far ahead—the first ninety days are usually the most critical time period in your employment with an organization.

4

Conquering
the First Ninety Days

The first ninety days in a new job will usually make or break us. Because organizations now expect that employees will not stay as long as has been typical in the past, they expect them to produce much more quickly. Often, long-term success and promotability are determined in the first three months on the job. For many organizations, the first ninety days are a probationary period to prove we are a fit for the company and for the role for which we've been selected.

> Serena received an offer in December of her senior year in college with a start date two weeks after her May graduation. Those five months were valuable time that Serena should have used to create a plan for herself to be successful in her new job. Instead, she enjoyed the last semester of college and did not turn her attention to preparing until a few days before her first day on the job. Creating a personal plan for success is an important part of keeping a job.
>
> Serena survived her first ninety days, but her career could have started off better and she likely would have

been promotable sooner had she prepared more intentionally for her first three months on the job.

The plan for the first ninety days can include several elements, such as learning more about the organizational culture, understanding the expectations of the role, familiarizing ourselves with customers and clients, building relationships with new coworkers, and setting goals for our performance.[1] There is not a second chance to make a first impression. It all begins with a plan.

What steps make for a great first ninety days on the job?

Dig Deep into Company Culture

Hopefully you understood the organizational culture well before you accepted the job. However, there are some things you really can't know until you start working. Beyond the corporate purpose, mission, and core values, it is important to learn how things get done in your organization as quickly as possible. Be a noticer, and observe who influences others on your team and in the organization and how they navigate the organization to achieve results. Making these kinds of observations will continue throughout your career, so learning how to do this early will be advantageous. Understanding how things get done is a big part of understanding the culture, which helps a new employee find success.

> When Tim accepted a sales position at a new company, he continued to work the same hours he did in his previous position, a nonexempt hourly paid role. He arrived right at 8:30 and was out the door promptly at 5:00. After a few weeks, he noticed that the other salespeople did not leave at 5:00. Finally, he asked one of his coworkers why they stayed late. He explained to Tim that the sales director, Brittney, always stayed late, and she valued both face time and people who didn't watch the clock.

At Tim's company, it was statistically true that those who worked a little later tended to be promoted more quickly than those who did not. Perhaps Brittney valued the work ethic, or maybe those who put in a few extra minutes each day achieved more sales and contributed more to the start-up they were growing. Whatever the case, Tim caught on quickly and began putting in the few extra hours that were part of his company culture, and he was successful in his new role.

Understand the Expectations of Your Supervisor

The relationship with your new boss is the most critical element of success in your new job. When you were selected for the role, you were likely given a job description. Now it is time to understand what success looks like in your job. Ask your new boss that very question, and ask others too. What measurable goals are you expected to achieve in the first ninety days and the first year of employment? Who are the key stakeholders with whom you need to focus relationship-building efforts? How does your boss prefer that you communicate—in person, phone, email, text? How often does your boss want you to communicate your results? How does your boss prefer to give feedback and how often? What are your boss's expectations about the hours you work? Is it preferred that you work in the office, or is working off-site accepted?

Learn Professionalism

Regardless of how casual a work environment is, there are still important unwritten rules to follow. In the first ninety days, pay attention to the behaviors of others to discern what is acceptable and what is not in your organization. There are a few personal boundaries that should be adopted regardless of where you work or your role.

Never Ever Talk Badly about the Boss, Your Teammates, Your Clients, or Your Organization

In fact, it is a good policy to avoid all trash talk about anyone, except maybe your least favorite sports team. Eventually, whatever you say is going to get back to the people you talk about, and then your reputation is ruined. People won't trust you, especially your boss. In those circumstances, it's hard to keep a job and certainly difficult to grow a career. Guard your reputation because once you have lost it, you can rarely get it back.

Don't Wait to Be Told What to Do

Early in your career, adopt the question, "What can I do to help you?" If you finish your assignments, look around and ask others how you can help. When you see a coworker stressed and overwhelmed, ask how you can help them over the hump. Look for opportunities to solve a problem or take on a task that needs to be handled.

For the most part, I credit success in my own career to noticing a need and assuming the responsibility. Early on, my company was just a little bigger than a start-up. There was a lot of work to be done but not many people to do it. We were working hard to build systems and processes to meet the needs of an ever-growing business. Roles were less defined, and the cultural norm was "If you see something that needs to be done, then do it. It is better to ask forgiveness than permission." Leaders have little time to tell people what to do. If they have to find work for you to do, they might decide they don't really need you. Take ownership of adding value.

Own Your Mistakes

When you make a mistake, admit it and ask for help to correct it. When you are learning a new job, mistakes are inevitable, and they are important in helping you learn. Leaders trust and respect employees who are transparent and don't try to cover up their errors. Usually, covering them up makes things much worse.

Owning mistakes is more difficult in a fear-based culture than in a people-centered culture. In one of my early career jobs, I worked for a very difficult boss. She had zero leadership skills but excellent berating and belittling skills. I was petrified of making a mistake. But even in that atmosphere, covering up a mistake would only warrant even harsher treatment. Later, I worked for an organization that understood that making mistakes was a vital part of the learning process and that freedom from the fear of making a mistake helps employees grow in collaboration and trust of one another. Mistakes can happen at any time during a career, but they needn't be career limiting. Look for more thoughts on this topic throughout the book.

Work Harder Than Anyone Else

As a new employee, simply exhibiting a willingness to work hard at everything you do helps you to immediately establish credibility with your supervisor, your team, and your organization. It's the one thing that is totally within your control.

Be the First to Arrive and the Last to Leave

Make it your policy to be the first to arrive and the last to leave, not just to work but to everything—meetings, company dinners, conference calls, and so on. Early in your career, you do have to prove yourself. You may be the most talented person on your team or in your organization, but until you produce results, your talent is not as valuable. Prove your commitment by putting in the time on the job and being willing to do what others are unwilling to do.

One of my clients shared the example of one of her emerging leaders. She supervised a young man destined to be a senior leader in the organization because he is a relative of the owner. What impressed her most about this young man was that even though his future was all but guaranteed, he made sure he was the hardest working member of the team. He was the first to arrive and the last to leave. He was tenacious in meeting expectations, and he did whatever it took to achieve results for himself and his team. His work ethic created respect and followership before he assumed his first leadership position. It can do the same for you.

Take Care of Yourself

There is no better time to start developing good habits to keep you mentally, physically, emotionally, and spiritually healthy than right from the beginning. Taking care of yourself will help you not only to excel right from the start of your new job but also to stay healthy to keep your job and grow your career over time. We all know that exercising, eating healthy, getting enough sleep, taking time to pray or meditate, reading, and spending time with friends and family are important to physical, mental, spiritual, and emotional health. What we struggle with is committing the time and maintaining the discipline to do them.

When we are just beginning our careers, we think we have unlimited capacity and can do without sleep and exercise and other healthy living habits. Later we learn the toll bad habits take on our body, mind, and spirit. I regret that I did not make this a priority earlier in my own career. I was decades into leadership and a mother of three before I changed my trajectory by deciding to take better care of myself.

The single most significant change I made to help me be a better leader, wife, parent, friend, volunteer, and more was to reserve one hour each day for myself. I did not recognize this need on my own. My leader had no doubt noticed the stress I was carrying and how it impacted my leadership, countenance, and influence. One day, he gave me some meaningful feedback: "I don't know what will work for you, but you need to take time every morning to prepare yourself before you arrive at work in order to be more positive."

That is really all he said, except for sharing with me the morning routine he used to prepare himself for the day.

Making the change was not easy. My morning routine was getting out of bed at the last possible minute, going directly to the shower, getting dressed quickly, and getting three little people ready and in the car for various drop-off points. Those days remind me of the commercial about the Marine Corps. I was doing more before 6:00 a.m. than most people did all day. Arriving at the office, I often skipped breakfast and dove right into the challenges of the day.

I knew that if I intended to grow my career, I needed to heed my boss's feedback. When my children were small, it meant I had to get up one hour before everyone else to have time to myself. I used that time to exercise, read something encouraging, and pray. My boss was right. The change in my habits set the tone for my day, and I became known as someone who was sometimes too positive!

Most of us will spend about forty years working. We must invest in taking care of our mind, body, and spirit to be effective and to enjoy the journey. The first ninety days on a job are the perfect time to start beneficial career-long habits that will serve you your entire career.

The first ninety days of any new job are critical. You never get a second chance to make a first impression, and that is exactly what the first ninety days are—a first impression. Once you have mastered the first ninety days, you are ready to start investing in other practices and habits that will help you keep your job and grow your career.

WHAT'S MY STORY?

1. What have I noticed about the habits and behaviors of my coworkers? What are some of the unwritten rules about behavior?

2. What are the expectations of my supervisor in my new role? Which expectations were expected? Which expectations are a surprise to me? Which ones require more understanding now that I am actually doing the job?

3. What areas of professionalism need my attention? What habits should I incorporate to be more professional? Which of my habits do I need to correct to be more professional?

4. What mistakes have I made in my first ninety days? What have I learned?

5. What habits am I incorporating into my daily routine to help me take good care of myself? What habits do I need to cultivate? What trade-offs do I need to make to carve out the time to take good care of myself?

5

Managing Relationships

The reality of life is that success at anything begins with relationships. Volumes upon volumes have been written about this subject to help people thrive in their families, friendships, communities, and at work. Without mastering the art of managing relationships with our coworkers, clients, and leaders, our career growth is extremely limited.

Healthy relationships begin with a healthy heart. There is a saying that "hurt people hurt people." Whoever we are, our past successes, childhood experiences, and traumatic events all become part of who we are in the workplace. If we work forty hours per week for forty years, it is impossible to keep past and present struggles from impacting us at work. If we have been hurt, it is highly likely we will take that hurt into our career, and the impact of that hurt on us can impact others around us. Recognizing this truth, it is incredibly important to examine our hearts and do everything possible to make them whole.

> Ryan graduated from a prominent business school at the top of his class. He won numerous awards and surpassed

even his own high expectations. After several internships during college and grad school at prestigious organizations, he was recruited by one of the top consulting firms in the country and paid a six-figure salary at twenty-five years of age. From the outside, by every measure, Ryan exuded success. Unfortunately, his academic success and previous experience did not result in a successful start to his career. The primary reason was that he began his career in poor emotional health, and he could not manage his relationships with his boss, coworkers, and clients. You could say he had an unhealthy heart. His lack of self-confidence and self-esteem manifested itself in perfectionism. When he found he could not be perfect on the job, it gave way to anxiety. The anxiety paralyzed him, which destroyed his performance.

The firm placed Ryan under a leader known for strong people skills, but unfortunately Kent was located in a different city. Not only did Kent fail to provide early career guidance to Ryan, but he saw so little of Ryan that he had no idea his young employee was struggling so much. One look at Ryan and the deep dark circles under his eyes, his pale skin, and his significant weight loss should have been signals that something was deeply wrong.

As talented as he was, Ryan could not overcome his emotional-health issues, and it eventually cost him his job. Poor emotional health impacts relationships not only on the job but also in every area of our lives. What could Ryan have done differently? First, he could have sought professional help to work through the issues that caused his low self-esteem and perfectionism. Then he could have changed some of his behaviors as a result of healing his heart.

Of all the reasons I have seen people fail in their career, by far the most common is the inability to build positive and productive relationships in the workplace. As a leader working through relationship issues with my employees, I found that in almost every single case, the root of the problem was a hurting heart.

Sometimes I provided feedback to an employee about the behaviors I and others observed. The employee would begin furiously taking notes about what he could change in his behavior to result in a different impact. However, a heart cannot be healed by checking items off a list of new behaviors. It goes much deeper than simply willing yourself to change.

If you find yourself in this situation, seek help. Whether it is through the company's employee assistance program, private counseling, or a pastor, find someone to help you peel back the layers. From my own experience and from observing others, I have found that if the heart is healed, appropriate behaviors will follow. You won't need a checklist.

Building solid relationships is the most important factor in keeping a job and growing a career. Take care of heart issues early so that they do not negatively impact your career. Don't try to solve them by yourself. Ask for help when you need it.

Be Self-Aware

Self-awareness means understanding the difference between our intent and our impact. If we are emotionally healthy people, most everything we do is intended for good. Generally, no one starts out with the intent to hurt, annoy, or frustrate other people. In fact, when it happens, we are often completely surprised to learn that our impact was very different from our intention.

In a virtual working world, this is even more difficult. If most of the interaction between you and your team is on-screen, intentions can easily be misconstrued and relationships damaged. With the lack of person-to-person interaction, you might not even know there is a relationship issue.

One of my favorite books is *Integrity: The Courage to Meet the Demands of Reality* by Dr. Henry Cloud. In the book, he helps us understand the difference between our intent and our impact by examining the effect of a wake left behind a boat. When a boat slices through the water, it leaves behind a wake. As we pursue the desired results, we also need to be conscious about the wake we leave behind in the way we treat other people. To be successful in building relationships, a good team member must care about not only *what* is accomplished but also *how* it is accomplished.

Dr. Cloud states it clearly: "The wake is the results we leave behind. And the wake doesn't lie and it doesn't care about excuses. It is what it is. No matter what we try to do to explain why, or to justify what the wake is, it still remains. It is what we leave behind and is our record."[1] To the people you work with, your intent is not very important. Regardless of how hard you tried to do the right thing or what you thought was most helpful, all they will remember and know is your impact.

Being self-aware means understanding and having keen insight into your personality, including strengths and weaknesses, values and beliefs, your emotions, and your purpose. Healthy self-awareness helps you accurately read other people and understand how they perceive you. If you have insight into these perceptions, you can modify your behavior to leave the desired impact.

This is an essential skill if you want to establish and grow effective relationships in the workplace. How can you become more self-aware? Following are a few recommendations:

- *Take personality and psychometric assessments and receive feedback.* These assessments range from simple ones online to complex ones administered by a psychologist. Choose which to take based on the depth you think is appropriate compared to the financial investment you are willing to make. Check with the talent or human resources department within your organization to see what they offer and if they have resources to provide feedback. Some of my favorite assessments to help with self-awareness are DISC, Judgment Index, Birkman,

Myers-Briggs Type Indicator, Strengthfinders, and Hogan. There are many choices, but the most important part of the process is to receive and review the feedback.

- *Think about the feedback and what it means.* Receiving personality assessment or psychometric test results can be overwhelming. Don't simply skim over them. After all, this is about the way your mind works, which is important to understand if you want to have the most effective impact on others. Consider even a full weekend personal retreat to read through the assessments, understanding exactly what is measured and what the results mean.

- *Set goals for behavioral change.* Based on what you learn from the feedback, set specific behavioral-change goals and write them down. I recommend that you choose only two or three behaviors to work on at a time. It takes a lot of work and repetition for true behavioral change. Trying to do too much too fast can derail your effort.

- *Select trusted friends with whom to share results and seek feedback.* This is the most difficult step because it requires vulnerability. However, it can be the most helpful step. Choose your most trusted advisors and share your results, personal insights, and goals. Ask them if you are on target. Ask them what they would add for you to consider for personal growth. As you begin to make changes, continue to ask for feedback as to how you are progressing from their points of view.

- *Seek feedback at work.* Ask your supervisors, teammates, and even those you supervise to give you feedback about your progress. You might not receive the absolute truth from some of these people at first, but as you build trust and express vulnerability, others will expand their feedback to you. If your organization uses a 360 degree feedback tool to gather anonymous feedback from all angles, that might help you receive the feedback you need.

Building self-awareness was one of my early challenges. It took me awhile to realize I did not have it, and it took me even longer to do something about it. Engaging a coach really helped me to sort through feedback and identify behaviors to make me a more effective leader. I admire the emerging leaders I see who are self-aware and have a propensity to develop behaviors that leave a positive impact. Developing self-awareness is a skill to be honed and one we use throughout our careers to help us effectively manage relationships.

Grow Trust

Once we have improved our self-awareness, a natural by-product is the ability to grow trust. From the beginning of our careers, it is important to grow trust with our boss, coworkers, and teammates. If we start out building trust, by the time we grow into positions of leadership, we will be experienced in building trust with direct reports.

In today's uncertain climate, we see the level of trust people have in leaders in business and political arenas declining rapidly. In his bestselling book, *The Speed of Trust*, leadership author and speaker Stephen M. R. Covey explains what leaders must do to recover trust: "One of the fastest ways to restore trust is to make and keep commitments, even very small ones, to ourselves and others."[2] Doing what you say you will do builds trust in not only professional relationships but personal ones too.

Trusting others frightens some people. But without trust, organizations cannot thrive and prosper. A lack of trust pits us against one another and destroys morale, culture, and innovation. An organization with a lack of trust among its members is often characterized as competitive instead of collaborative. Such conditions are a threat to a healthy future. Without trust, it is impossible to build and maintain healthy relationships.

Trust matters. Whether it is between two people in a marriage, a friendship, or a working relationship or among employees in an organization, trust is crucial. Team members who trust one another, their leader, and the organization are one of the most valuable components of individual, team, and organizational success.

In the past, leadership development focused on issues such as developing leadership skills, doing the right things to climb the ladder and gain authority, and competing for positions of power within an organization. Human resource departments screened for personality traits that indicated talent with the potential to lead and inspire others. However, the world has changed.

What you have achieved in the past and your positional authority rapidly depreciate in a world lacking values, integrity, and respect for authority. Instead, your ability to persuade others, most of whom you have no authority over, to join a collaborative effort around a common purpose and goal is the key. That key is named trust.

An integral element in establishing trust with coworkers, managers, and clients is possessing a good reputation or a good name. A good name implies word-of-mouth trustworthiness. A trustworthy person is someone who possesses the integrity and confidence to build strong relationships and inspire others to accomplish amazing things.

In times of war, soldiers are forced to put trust in their leaders. Their very lives depend on the decisions their leaders make. Commanding officers must earn the trust of their soldiers long before they step onto the battlefield together. If they don't, it is possible to lose the support of the troops with the first missile fired.

Perhaps the greatest example of someone earning trust and becoming trustworthy comes from the Bible in the Old Testament book of Judges. Her name was Deborah, and she was the only female judge in all of Israel. She lived in an era when the ceiling wasn't glass. It was cast iron and bronze and low. We read in Judges 17:6, "In those days Israel had no king; everyone did as they saw fit." Deborah stood in opposition to the downward spiral. She had a good name and the trust that went along with it.

In the story, Israel found itself under siege from the armies of Jabin and with no way to defend itself. Jabin sent Sisera, his commander, to Israel with troops, weapons, shields, and chariots far more advanced than anyone in the region possessed.

Deborah, an autonomous leader, trusted God in a time when governmental infrastructure did not exist. She sent out and summoned a man named Barak. We know that Deborah was a trusted leader because Barak was willing to make the seventy-mile journey simply at her request. When Barak arrived, she shared a goal, a mission, and a purpose with him: to conquer Jabin and his commander Sisera and their vast army.

Deborah directed Barak to command ten thousand men from atop Mt. Tabor. He agreed to do so, but only if she accompanied him into battle. That's trust and admiration. Barak had no doubt about the truth of her words, nor did he fear the enemy. We also know that God trusted Deborah because he told her how the story would end. Deborah told Barak that they would be victorious and that a woman would be the one to ultimately kill Sisera.

Barak trusted Deborah, and Deborah trusted Barak. She went with him into battle, and his men annihilated Sisera's troops to the last man. The sole survivor was Sisera. Just as Deborah said, Sisera died from a Bedouin woman's tent spike through his head. Deborah did not let down those who trusted her. She trusted God, and God found her to be a most trustworthy leader.

The key to relationships today is trust and trustworthiness. When you possess integrity and an understood and well-communicated set of values, there's no room for selfish motives or power-hungry intentions. Developing trust with others requires the following specific behaviors:

- Always do what you say you will do.
- Never lie.
- Keep confidences.
- Be transparent.

- Apologize when necessary.
- Share the credit.
- Be consistent.
- Show humility.
- Express compassion.
- Practice kindness.

These ten practices will help you grow trust with your boss, your teammates, and your clients. Trust is a treasured gift. Protect it and you will develop meaningful relationships that will help you keep your job and grow your career.

Listen Well

The late author Stephen Covey wrote a life-changing book called *The 7 Habits of Highly Effective People*. Habit 5 changed my life, truly: "Seek first to understand and then be understood."[3]

When we are in a conversation, how often are we more focused on what we will say next than on what the other person is saying? The best communicators are not those who have a vast vocabulary and superior oration skills. The best communicators are the great listeners. They respond to what is being said rather than thinking about what to say next.

To be a great listener, we must close the computer, put down the mobile device, clear our mind of distractions, and look the other person directly in the eye. A good listener listens not only with his ears but also with his whole body. Leaning in, continuous eye contact, taking notes, and responsive facial expressions are all indications of being a good listener. These behaviors will also result in hearing the other person well and responding in a more informed way.

Great listeners are curious people who ask many questions. They are curious about other people and how they think. Effective listeners ask clarifying questions and even ask questions that help the other person process their ideas.

The second part of Covey's fifth habit is equally as important. While we need to be good listeners, we also need to be sure we are clearly understood. The formula is simple: listen, repeat back what you heard, and then respond to what you heard. Sometimes we say, "I am just making sure we are on the same page." Practice this skill repeatedly, and it will lead to becoming a better listener and strengthened relationships in the workplace.

Pay Attention

We live in a world full of distractions. Some of them are by choice, and others are generated by the society in which we live. Even in writing a book, which takes enormous focus, there are numerous distractions. Email and social media notifications and upcoming calendar events pop up on the screen if not disabled. Spam calls ring our phones, and delivery people ring our doorbells. Our world is continuously in motion and constantly distracting us.

Think about the last virtual or in-person meeting you attended. How many times did someone glance at a mobile device, step out to take a phone call, or just mentally check out because of a brewing crisis? Even while bingeing on Netflix or Hulu, many of us are multitasking by texting with friends, surfing the net, shopping online, or scrolling our social media news feed. Every few minutes a news alert goes off on our devices, reminding us of the fragility of our world as a volcano erupts, a virus spreads globally, or a forest fire destroys a mountainside. It is simply difficult to pay attention to anyone or anything if we do not intentionally focus.

During my career, I have spent a lot of time on airplanes. To me, the best part of flying is that I can turn off the world for the duration of the flight. I can choose not to connect to the unreliable onboard Wi-Fi. I can turn off the TV screen in front of me, and I can disconnect from the people around me by putting on the universal "I don't want to talk" device—my noise-canceling ear-buds. An airplane trip provides time for me to read a book, write a blog post, or even generate a strategic plan for next year. It is a precious few hours of time to focus. We all need that kind of focus.

Sometimes we need to be undistracted in a different way. We need to focus on the people around us. When we fail to keep our head up and notice other people, we miss opportunities to build relationships. This was a lesson I learned a couple of years ago on an airplane.

She was young, thin, and blonde—the stereotype of everyone I feel surrounded by these days and a representation of what I once was. She bebopped down the airplane aisle, the energy exuding from her when she plopped down in the seat next to me. After helping her find the charger port under her seat, she said, "Thank you, ma'am."

Ugh. "Ma'am." She was incredibly polite, but I suddenly felt ancient. I quickly surmised that she was a twenty-something who saw me as a "has been." I was so wrong. We both put in our earbuds and drifted off to our private spaces. She was listening to music, and I was listening to nothing. It was simply my signal that I did not want to talk.

After takeoff, we both removed our earbuds and began clearing our laps. We looked at each other in that knowing way that we were both preparing to head to the bathroom as soon as the "fasten seat belt" sign was turned off. Ever the strategist, I told her I would go to the lavatory in the first-class cabin, and she could go to the one in the rear. She asked, "They won't attack you for using the first-class lavatory?" "No," I told her. "I've got this." With great confidence, I sprinted through the first-class cabin without slowing down. The key is to perfect the look that if I am stopped it might result in an unpleasant experience for everyone.

Returning to our seats, the young lady and I had bonded over the bathroom experience. She was impressed with my confidence, and I was intrigued with her personality. Her vibe was electric and her smile was contagious, and all of the sudden I was not so interested in putting my earbuds back in my ears. I wanted to know more about this young woman.

We introduced ourselves and began talking. Bethany shared a difficult human-resources challenge at work. I helped her think about solutions, and she helped me think about my next book—the one you are reading right now. A few minutes into the conversation, I realized that she is a brilliant young woman. Very curious, she asked about my work and started taking notes of my recommended reading suggestions.

When I shared the focus of my next book, she gave me several topics to include based on her own experiences. By the time we landed, I was ready to hammer out six chapters, and she was prepared for an upcoming meeting. We did work together in those ninety minutes.

Before deplaning, I signed a copy of my recently released book *Bet on Talent: How to Create a Remarkable Culture That Wins the Hearts of Customers* and gave it to Bethany because I knew she would read it. She contacted me on social media an hour later to show me a photo depicting that her boss had already ordered fifteen copies.

Nice stories should always be followed by a lesson to learn. This is it in a message to myself: Girl (or ma'am), take your earbuds out! I almost missed what could have been a divine appointment because I wasn't paying attention. I almost missed this bright, insightful, confident, connected, and wise-beyond-her-years incredible young woman because I wanted my ninety minutes of focused quiet time, unwilling to pay attention to someone next to me.

Reflecting on the interaction, I considered the women sitting on either side of Bethany that day on the plane. One of us had an amazing experience; the other one kept her earbuds in her ears. The lady in the window seat was so close to growing right along with us, but she missed the opportunity, having completely ignored us for the duration of the flight.

I am thankful to have met Bethany. My life was enriched in those ninety minutes, and I am encouraged to have met someone who will be a world changer in her generation. So my advice is this: the next time you sit down on a plane, think about taking your earbuds out. Discover what you might receive and give and what relationships you might create because you paid attention.

To keep a job and grow a career, invest in relationships with people inside and outside the organization. Doing so will yield dividends that will not only help you be successful but also make the journey much more fun. Building meaningful relationships at work and elsewhere is a lifelong pursuit. If you are willing to turn these principles into habits, you will find tremendous return on your investment.

WHAT'S MY STORY?

1. What personality assessments have I taken? What did I learn from them? Who could offer me more feedback?

2. What is the one habit I want to change to become more self-aware?

3. Who could I trust to provide meaningful feedback about my blind spots?

4. What habits could I incorporate into daily life to make me a more trustworthy person?

5. Where am I not paying attention to those around me—at work? On my team? At home? What distractions do I need to eliminate to be a better listener and pay better attention to others?

6

Managing Your Performance

Early in my career, I remember being told, "This is a do-it-yourself company." The leader who shared that statement with me was encouraging me to take responsibility for both my performance and my development. In general, I think organizations and leaders have grown to understand that while employees must manage their performance and development, they need leaders who will encourage and support their efforts.

No one is more invested in your career than you are, and the most important daily task you have in order to keep your job and prepare you for any role in the future is to manage your performance. Managing your performance is the process of understanding expectations, setting goals based on those expectations, and receiving feedback about whether you are meeting those expectations.

Understand Ongoing Expectations

In an earlier chapter, I talked about the importance of understanding your manager's expectations in the first ninety days.

Those kinds of discussions with your boss do not end after the first one. Hopefully, they occur frequently, ensuring that you know what the goals are and what your role is in meeting those goals.

If your supervisor does not initiate regular conversations about expectations, you can always suggest a schedule that works for both of you. Many organizations discuss expectations on a quarterly basis. Some do this monthly. Early in your job, you might need more frequent engagement with your boss. However, as you learn more about the company and your role, you will be expected to need less day-to-day direction and grow your capability to direct your own activities and achieve results.

Set Performance Goals

When I was younger, I really wanted to play the piano. I imagined myself in Carnegie Hall sitting down at a baby grand piano in a long flowing evening gown with my hair in an "updo" decorated with rhinestones and my long slender fingers with perfectly manicured nails gliding across the keys and playing concertos from Bach, Mozart, and Chopin. It seemed like such a simple process: select an excellent piano teacher, go to lessons every Tuesday afternoon after school, and get accepted to the Juilliard School in New York, and I would be on my way to international fame as a concert pianist.

We know that no worthwhile goal is achieved that simply. My desire to become a concert pianist broke down somewhere between selecting the piano teacher and learning to play with both hands. Seriously, I took piano lessons for four years without ever playing with both hands at the same time! Here is where I went wrong: becoming a concert pianist was a vision, not a goal. I needed to set goals to achieve the vision. The goals provide the milestones we need to accomplish on our way to achieving the vision. Without goals, the journey just becomes a lot of wandering in the wilderness.

My piano teacher set clear expectations. She instructed me to practice every day for thirty minutes. Today there are some great apps to help track piano practice time. When I was learning, I had a little red booklet to record my time each day, and at my lesson I received a sticker for completed practice time. What kept me from achieving the vision? I didn't have enough stickers in my little red books.

The goal was specific, measurable, actionable, realistic, and time bound. Practice thirty minutes each day every week. Given my level of talent, had I met the goal, I probably still would never have been a concert pianist. We will never know. However, I am sure that if I had met the expectations of my teacher by achieving the practice goals, I would be able to play with both hands simultaneously today.

Along with understanding the expectations of your role, you and your boss will need to set goals for results and for your personal performance. Usually, the goals are cascaded from company goals to division goals to team goals to individual goals. If it is not clear to you how your individual role supports the company objectives, ask other people to help you make that connection. Understanding how you contribute to organizational success makes your work more meaningful and helps you understand your worth to the organization.

The goals you set should be specific to what you are expected to accomplish. If they are too broad, it will be difficult to focus on what you need to do. Goals are only meaningful if they are measurable, so be sure you can measure your accomplishment of the goals. Any goal you agree to should be actionable. Theoretical goals are rarely achieved. The goals you choose should be realistic and attainable. It's good to create goals that stretch you, but in managing your own performance they should not be out of reach. Lastly, your goals should be time bound with clear time frames and deadlines.

Receive Timely Feedback

Everyone needs and deserves feedback. When we receive feedback about how well we did something, we know to repeat that behavior. Conversely, when we are given feedback about underperforming, that helps us to know the adjustments to make. Great leaders are masters at giving feedback, not just in formal performance reviews but also in daily coaching.

If you have ever been part of an athletic team, you have likely experienced that kind of coaching. A baseball coach breaks down every element of a player's swing or pitch to help the player improve. Together, they work on the smallest of details to make incremental improvements. The same is true with dance coaches and vocal coaches. It's those small adjustments that can help us make exponential progress. We need the same kind of coaching and feedback to be successful in our jobs as well. A good leader is a good coach who helps team members make incremental improvements that yield positive gains for the individual team member and the entire team.

Unfortunately, we sometimes have a leader who provides little regular feedback or even no feedback at all. How do you ask for feedback from that kind of boss? It's a delicate dance of getting exactly what you need without being perceived as needy.

If you and your boss have regularly scheduled meetings, try to honor that time to receive feedback. After all, your boss likely has other people to supervise and many projects of their own to complete. However, if you think you are off track or need specific direction to keep things moving, you should not hesitate to ask for help. The primary job of a leader is to lead, and that includes helping you stay on task to complete your goals. When desiring additional feedback, send an email requesting a time that is convenient. Your email might look like this:

> Is there a time this week that we could chat? I would appreciate your feedback on the project that is due the

end of the month. I am sure you are busy, so please let me know when a brief conversation would be convenient for you.

Your boss may be available right then. However, this approach assures you do not interrupt at an inconvenient time.[1]

Once the time to speak is set up, it is important to be prepared with specific questions. If your boss does not have a template for casual, intermittent feedback, you can offer one. Your boss may actually be grateful for the help. The questions might look like the following:

- Is my current rate of progress toward goals meeting your expectations?
- Why or why not?
- What would you like me to do more or less of as I complete this project?
- Are there any behaviors you have observed that might prevent me from achieving these goals?
- What is one result or behavior you would like for me to focus on for the next thirty days?
- How can I add more value to the team on this project?

When I led my own team, a few of my direct reports were very astute about getting my attention and feedback, which helped them achieve their goals. They sent me updates on their work and a list of their questions twenty-four hours before our meetings. The timing was perfect. It was not so far in advance that it was lost in my inbox but still gave me enough time to review and think about the conversation before we met. It enabled me to give them my complete focus during our time together and to be sure we focused on what they needed most to be effective and successful.

Respond to Negative Feedback

If you work long enough, you will eventually receive some kind of negative feedback. None of us are perfect. It is likely that the negative feedback will fall in the range between being so vague you have to read between the lines to find the intent and so harsh that you have to survive the shock. Your ability to keep a job and grow a career can depend on your ability to receive, process, and respond to negative feedback.

> Rebecca was enjoying an amazing career. She was a hard charger and overachiever. The team leaders particularly appreciated her work ethic. She ran circles around the other members of her team. Still, she had blind spots, particularly in the way she interacted with the rest of the team. Impatience was her trademark emotion, and everyone on the team became tense when she was wound up, ignoring the details and charging through team decisions.
>
> The team and her boss tried to give Rebecca feedback about her negative impact. Her behavior, while distracting, was not detrimental to her career. However, her inability to respond and recover from negative feedback was sabotaging all the success she enjoyed. When faced with negative feedback, she often became defensive and emotional, blaming others and making excuses. Eventually, her responses shut her boss and her team down, and she was not given any feedback at all. It would only be a matter of time before hardworking and hard-charging Rebecca would derail her own career.

Let's learn from Rebecca's failure and set ourselves up to appropriately respond to negative feedback, which will eventually help us succeed. It may not feel like it at the time, but feedback is a gift. Acknowledging that fact helps us to accept feedback and make needed changes.[2]

The following steps will help you receive and respond appropriately to negative feedback:

- *Don't just listen but hear what the person giving you feedback is really saying.* Don't interrupt; allow them to provide the feedback. It can be very difficult to give someone negative feedback. Take notes of questions you want to ask, but allow the person to finish before saying anything.

- *Don't feel compelled to respond immediately.* If you feel overly emotional, hurt, or angry, suggest that you take some time to think about the feedback and come back at another time to go more in depth. Recognize your emotions and avoid venting to coworkers or, even worse, on social media. Such actions can wreck your career.

- *Ask clarifying questions.* If you don't understand, ask for examples. Be sure to ask in a way that does not sound defensive but is a genuine desire to comprehend. A good way to start is, "Tell me more about . . ."

- *As you begin to understand, make affirming statements.* For example, you might say, "I understand the expectation better" or "Your feedback provides me more clarity."

- *Don't make excuses.* Focus less on why you did what you did and more on what you will change going forward. Even say out loud, "Going forward, I will try to . . ." to confirm that you understand expectations.

- *Thank the person for being a truth teller.* Truth tellers are gold in your professional life. If you are fortunate enough to find one, thank them in person and in a follow-up note.

- *Validate the feedback.* Share the feedback with your most trusted advisors and mentors and ask them to help you process it. They can help you overcome the emotionalism and move on to resolution.

- *Make the changes you can and move on.* Do not wallow in negative feedback. The value in critical feedback is to enable you to make changes to be successful. Do not make it more than it is. Often, people are actually recognized more for the performance adjustments they make than for their performance in areas of natural ability. Adaptability and resilience are important leadership capabilities and are often identified in adversity.

Anyone who wants to keep a job and grow a career will face negative feedback at one time or another. The most successful people understand how to receive it and respond to it in productive ways. They understand that knowing the truth is the only way to improve, and they are thankful for the truth tellers.

Prepare for a Promotion or New Opportunity

The best time to prepare for a new opportunity is before it happens. Over the course of your career, opportunities for new roles, promotions, and new jobs at other companies will come at unexpected times. If you wait to prepare until the opportunity appears, you have waited too long. One of the great secrets of success is to be ready when an opportunity presents itself. While we can envision and sometimes predict what might happen in the future, opportunity rarely announces that it is coming until it knocks on our door.

> Renée was ready for opportunity when it came along. The reality was that she had all but given up that her employer would notice her leadership abilities. For years, she went unnoticed while performing a transactional role for her organization. Her teammates recognized her talent and often sought her wisdom and counsel, but the leadership of the company completely overlooked her. At the time, they pursued people they saw as more charismatic to promote into leadership positions.

Instead of becoming bitter because she was ignored, Renée focused on continuing to grow and prepare herself not so much for an opportunity in her current organization but to be ready if she received an offer somewhere else. She focused her development plan on growing her leadership skills and selected a coach to help her. While she had very little leadership responsibility at work, she volunteered to serve on nonprofit boards, chairing several. These assignments allowed her to grow in her leadership ability and to try out some skills before being in the spotlight within her company.

While it did not happen overnight, the most unexpected thing happened for Renée. There was a change in leadership within the organization, and the new leader sought a different persona and skill set for his leadership team members. He began to ask questions, and the answers led him to Renée. Much to everyone's surprise, including Renée's, he chose her for the new leadership assignment. She rose to the occasion, and because she was prepared when the opportunity came along, it was not many years before she was promoted again. In fact, eventually, she rose to a top position in the company.

For every story like Renée's, I could tell you ten more of people who were not ready when an opportunity came along. Some were busy complaining that no one was helping them get ahead. Others simply were not motivated enough to prepare themselves. A few did not take advantage of opportunities presented and were not given a second chance.

There are specific actions you can take to prepare for a promotion or another opportunity, ones that can change your career trajectory:

- *Increase your visibility.* This can be tricky, so make it about the work instead of about you. You want your work and your capabilities to become more visible in the organization.

Volunteer for project teams and special assignments, even if it means a little extra work for a season. This is a great way for leaders in the organization who are outside of your function to learn about you. If your organization offers volunteer service days, then join in and meet some new people.

- *If you are offered a development opportunity, take it, even if it is inconvenient.* Unless there are personal mitigating circumstances that make it impossible, take the course, go to the class, make the trip, and affirmatively respond to every opportunity offered. Midcareer, I had an amazing opportunity to attend the Advanced Management Program (AMP) at Harvard Business School. It is a very elite opportunity, but it does require being away from home for nine weeks. At the time, I had a freshman in college, a freshman in high school, and a nine-year-old. All of them were in critical seasons for one reason or another, and I knew my being away and not very accessible was going to be hard on the entire family. While it was difficult, we managed, and it turned out to be one of the very best development opportunities both personally and professionally. Everyone must decide for themselves the sacrifices they are willing to make, but if you are serious about being prepared for unexpected opportunities, then take the ones right in front of you.

- *Build your skills in roles outside of work.* Just like Renée, you can polish skills for a future role in a capacity other than your job. Volunteer, serve on a board, teach a class, coach a team, or join a club to build specific skills (such as Toastmasters for public speaking). All these "outside of work" activities and roles can help prepare you for an unexpected opportunity at work.

Following these actions can help you not only to keep your job and grow your career but also to take advantage of unexpected opportunities within your organization or elsewhere.

Know Your Worth

Whether you are searching for your first job, looking for another job, or expecting better pay in your current position, negotiation skills will be needed. Negotiating a starting salary or requesting a raise is difficult for most people. But becoming skilled at salary negotiation early on is important for your long-term career—the longer it takes to become proficient, the more money you will have left lying on the table throughout your career.

The first step in any salary negotiation is to know what you want. Then you must be able to make a case for that salary. Start by researching what people with your job responsibilities earn. There are many tools available that provide this information. Glassdoor, Monster.com, and Dice are among many sites that offer salary calculators.

Once you have identified the range of salaries for roles such as yours, consider the benefits included in your new job or included in your current job if requesting a raise. Be sure the ranges you research are comparing overall packages and not just salary. The sources you consult will usually also factor in geographic location and cost of living.

Here are some tips for negotiating a starting salary:

- Before you interview with any organization, do your research and know your expected salary range.
- Be cautious when comparing your expectations to what is posted about an organization at online job sites. They are often inaccurate, and it is better to discuss this with the recruiter or interviewer.
- Wait for the interviewer to discuss salary. In a market where jobs are plentiful, the interviewer is likely to discuss it at the first interview. During a time when jobs are less plentiful, salary may not be discussed until later in the interviewing process.

- When the topic of salary is discussed, lead with the strengths you will bring to the role and the organization. Also, discuss your own research about the value of the job and the value of someone with your specific experience. Avoid comparing to your former salary. That will not put you in the strongest negotiation position, and you should expect to be paid fairly for the new role regardless of prior compensation.
- Separate the benefits discussion from salary. It is good to keep in mind the entire package, including insurance, wellness facilities, childcare assistance, tuition reimbursement, and relocation, but try to keep it separate from the salary negotiation.
- If an offer is extended during an interview, don't accept it on the spot. Let the interviewer know that you want to give careful consideration to the offer, and agree to a date when you will respond with an answer.
- It is usually safe to assume an offer is negotiable. Most everything is!

Requesting a raise can be a more difficult negotiation process. The leverage you possess is that you might leave your job if you don't receive more pay. This can be daunting to an employer if there is a labor shortage or if your role is particularly hard to replace. If the labor market is plentiful, the employer is less likely to feel compelled to meet your demands. Be keenly aware of the job market for your particular skill set before you make a request. Following are some other tips for requesting a raise:

- Choose your timing. Has the company had a good year? Is your organization experiencing a downturn? Have there been recent layoffs or early retirement packages offered? This makes a difference as to whether your request will be considered.

- When you ask for a raise, focus on the value you are adding to the organization, the team, and the role. Don't focus on what is fair. Advocate in such a way that your boss can clearly see how you are contributing to the organization's success.
- If it is impossible to offer you more salary, try to negotiate other ways of increasing your income. Is a bonus available for hitting certain goals? Are there more stock options available? If you are paid on commission, could your commission be increased? Look for the win-win with your employer if it is a job you truly care about keeping.
- Money is not the reason why most people leave a job. Working for a poor leader is the most common reason people give for leaving a job. If you work for a strong leader who helps develop you and you enjoy a healthy organizational culture, those attributes might be worth a little less money and should be considered if you don't receive the raise you are seeking.
- Sometimes, it is time to move on to something else. If you and the organization cannot find a middle ground that satisfies you both, you might have to change jobs to find the compensation you think you deserve. It's better to search for something else that meets your needs than to stay in a job and be disengaged because you feel inadequately compensated.

Liz was a top performer at her first job out of business school. She chose the organization because of its great culture and developmental opportunities. Out of all the jobs she interviewed for, she really clicked with her future boss, Chloe, and thought she would be an outstanding mentor for her. Her starting salary was competitive but not the highest offer she received. The highest offer included more travel than Liz wanted.

Eighteen months into the job, Liz had been recognized by her boss and the division vice president for her great work and her ability to solve complex problems. Her first annual raise had been no more than a cost-of-living raise, and Liz knew that the company would soon be considering raises again. She decided to go ahead and let Chloe know that she was expecting a bigger increase in the upcoming rounds of reviews. It takes a lot of courage and skill to ask for a raise, but Liz knew that if she did not advocate for herself, it was likely that no one would.

After doing her homework, Liz confirmed that she was already falling behind in earnings compared to others with her qualifications. Business was booming in her company and her particular industry, and they could ill afford to lose the skills Liz brought to the table, especially to a competitor. It would be difficult to replace her, and the customers she served would be impacted by her absence. While that gave her some good leverage, Liz needed to navigate the conversation carefully. She did not want her boss to feel backed into a corner and begrudgingly give her a raise to keep her from leaving. Instead, she hoped that her boss would gain a new perspective and advocate for Liz.

When she approached Chloe in a monthly one-on-one, she started by confirming Chloe's assessment of her performance. Chloe could not say enough good things about Liz and her outstanding performance against the goals they had set together eighteen months earlier. After assuring Chloe that she really enjoyed her role, Liz explained that she hoped her outstanding performance would translate into a more substantial raise during the upcoming raise cycle. Knowing the range of percentage increases that the company awards based on performance, Liz asked for the highest percentage increase available.

At first, Chloe was surprised by the request, but then she decided Liz had made her case. Chloe knew that if she wanted to keep Liz long enough for her to progress in the company, she would need to advocate for a substantial increase. Six months later, Liz received a significant increase more in line with the salaries being paid for the same role in other companies. Liz's ability to speak up for herself and navigate a difficult subject left a very positive impression on Chloe. It is likely that Liz's actions led to an accelerated career path for her because her management of her own salary indicated early leadership potential. It was a big win for Liz because she was able to continue to work for a boss and organization that she loved and to be paid her worth.

Negotiating salaries and requesting raises are certainly some of the more challenging on-the-job discussions. However, the difficult conversations don't end there. In the next chapter, we will discuss critical issues we must learn to manage to keep a job and grow a career.

WHAT'S MY STORY?

1. Now that I have been on the job for a while, what expectations am I still unclear about that warrant a discussion with my boss?

2. What goals do my boss and I need to set about my performance in my current role?

3. What feedback do I need to seek in my current role? How will I prepare myself for the potential of negative feedback?

4. What am I doing right now to prepare myself for an unexpected opportunity? How can I invest more in my own development to prepare me?

5. Do I know my own worth? What steps do I need to take to determine my worth?

7

Navigating Land Mines

During the course of a career, we find land mines everywhere. It's important that we learn early how to navigate them so that they don't derail us or prevent us from achieving success. Some of these land mines we can see coming, and some we would have never guessed we would step on. For those we can anticipate, if we prepare ourselves, we can spot them, deactivate them, and keep on the path toward achieving our personal and organizational goals.

Recover from Rejection

A few years ago, I was attending a conference and sat with Donna, a colleague from another company, at dinner. She shared a story about one of her team members, Kate. She was disturbed because Kate received some unfair and unwarranted criticism from a senior leader in the organization. She had evaluated the situation and was sure the criticism was not justified and invalid. Even more frustrating was the fact that the narrative seemed to be related more to inaccurate personal judgments about Kate rather than professional performance issues. It was evident that Donna was an advocate for her team member and was heartbroken about the misplaced criticism.

As we talked further, my colleague explained that the senior leader, Jay, insisted she move Kate to another role and that Kate no longer serve his team. It appeared Kate was doing an outstanding job in winning the confidence of other leaders, and the members of Jay's leadership team trusted her. The colleague asked me what I would do in the same situation.

I explained that even if I felt the senior leader was making a mistake, I would want to do what was in my team member's best interest and make the change. It appeared Kate had performed at her best and given a valiant effort but was ultimately still rejected by Jay. Later, after I returned home from the conference, Donna called to tell me that reluctantly and regretfully, she made the change.

Perhaps one of the most intense negative emotions we can experience is rejection. It's brutal to be dismissed by those you love and serve. For leaders, the most painful rejection is the loss of followership. For individual contributors, it's the loss of confidence by leadership and team members. Despite our best efforts, sometimes the very ones we are giving the effort to reject us.

Resilience is the antidote to rejection. All leaders at one time or another will experience rejection. How do you overcome it when it happens to you? How can you become more resilient?

- *Recognize that your identity is not in a title or a role or determined by the people you lead.* Your identity is the combination of your faith and your personal vision, purpose, mission, and values. When you experience rejection in the workplace, remember that you are so much more than an employee number, a name badge, and a title on an organizational chart. Finding your identity in your faith can help you easily find a place of refuge amid the criticism. Resilient people overcome rejection by grounding themselves in an identity deeper than merely a role at work.

- *Examine your heart for hurts that need to heal.* Remember the statement I quoted earlier in the book: "Hurt people hurt people"? Is there a behavior you are demonstrating that is causing rejection by your followers? Your intention may be very different from the impact you are having on others. When you realize there is a gap between intent and impact, you must consider your own behavior. What is the root of the behavior? Is there a hurt that needs healing so that your behavior reflects the impact and influence you intend? If so, do the hard work of healing the hurt, and the behavior will follow. Resilient people take care of their hearts.

- *Admit that the rejection may not be about you at all.* Most often, rejection reflects the character of the one rejecting you. This was the case for my colleague's employee. Accept that you will not be loved and appreciated by everyone, and expend your energy on those you can positively influence. Resilient people control what they can control and release what they cannot.

- *Seek feedback and support from your tribe.* Surround yourself with people who encourage you on your career journey, but don't be hesitant to hear from those who appear not to be supportive. You can learn from both. Ask others for feedback about how your words and actions impact them. Ask the question, "What is it like to be on the other side of me?" Allow them to speak truth into you and embrace the encouragement they offer. Resilient people seek and accept feedback and apply what they learn. Don't forget what you learned in the previous chapter about responding to negative feedback.

- *Accept that the rejection is painful, but don't wallow in it.* Grieve the loss of not meeting your own expectations or the expectations of others, and then rise above it to find your way forward. Resilient people do not get stuck in the negativity of rejection. They move on, learning from the experience but not carrying negative baggage with them.

A few months after the original conversation, I was passing through Chicago, where Donna is based, and we caught up over lunch. She invited Kate to join us. Prior to my arrival, she had told me Kate was now flourishing. Her resilience was not just an example to her leader but to others on the team as well. In fact, she quickly gained the trust and followership of her new team. They admired her for displaying all five of the characteristics of resilient people. Her resiliency is a signature character trait of her leadership.

I was very impressed by this young leader as she told me about the pivot she had made in her career in the new role. Few times have I ever heard of rejection in the workplace that was as severe and unwarranted as this example. Yet she responded with great grace under pressure and used the experience to catapult her into new opportunities.

It would have been easy, under the circumstances, to be discouraged by the rejection of a senior leader, but Kate wasn't. She could have easily been consumed with fear about her career options and professional future, but she wasn't. Instead, she was resilient. In her resilience, her influence multiplied.[1]

When faced with rejection, we have options. If we allow a rejection to define us, our influence will be limited. If we exercise resilience, we are far more likely to gain influence and followers, which helps us grow a career.

Learn from Mistakes

Earlier, I talked about the importance of owning mistakes. As we grow in our careers and our responsibilities increase, we must not only own our mistakes but also learn from them and share what we learn with others.

Early on a Saturday morning before a new book release, I opened social media and learned that one of my launch team members found an error in the advance reader copy of the book. It turned my stomach a little. Mistakes really bother me, especially when they are mine. The name of a friend who was also one of my endorsers was misspelled in the body of the book. My stomach knotted up. Misspelling someone's name feels dishonoring. I knew it would be corrected in the final version, but it still bothered me.

We all make mistakes, and it seems like I make some kind of mistake every day. Sometimes, it is a typo like the one in my book. Sometimes, it is words spoken that should have remained unspoken. Occasionally, it is a poor decision that shows a lack of sound judgment. In all these circumstances, mistakes can be important learning lessons. But before we learn, we must recover.

How do you recover from a mistake? Following are some steps you can take to learn from your errant actions:

- *If possible, apologize.* Sometimes, there is no one to apologize to or no way to deliver the apology. But when you can, the apology should fit the mistake. In the case of the misspelling and because she also had received the advance reader copy, I immediately reached out to my friend and told her about the mistake. I sincerely apologized and explained that I had already informed my publisher. I assured her that her name would be correct in the published version. She was incredibly gracious in her response.

  I remember another mistake from years ago. I was leaving the office late one fall afternoon. My mind was a million miles away on the work I had just left and the chores waiting for me at home. I did something inconsiderate and thoughtless because I wasn't paying attention. On the side of the driveway that exits the campus, one of the grounds maintenance staff had piled leaves he had blown off the road to the shoulder. He may have been working on those leaves all afternoon. On my way out, I didn't slow down, and those leaves blew everywhere. I could see his frustration in my rearview mirror. A simple apology would not suffice for this situation. It was time to make brownies! The next morning, I drove on to the campus and pulled my car over to the side of the main road where I saw him working. I told the young man how sorry I was for wrecking his day and gave him a peace offering of a pan of brownies. It worked! Even today when I see him, we still laugh about it. A sincere apology goes a long way in recovering from a mistake.

- *If possible, correct the error.* There are some mistakes we cannot correct. We cannot take back thoughtlessly spoken words. We can cause harm that can never be reversed. In the case of the misspelled name of my friend, I could not correct the name in the advance reader copy of the book, but I did make sure it was correct for the first release. When you can, it's important to make the right correction.

Years ago, my oldest son achieved a special academic award at school. He had worked very hard for two years to earn the recognition. It was significant to him and to us. On the night of the awards banquet, I opened the program and his name was not included for the award. He was disappointed and so was I. After a few minutes of thinking about what to do, I walked up to one of the school administrators and asked about the omission. Instead of apologizing, she said, "Well, we don't proofread these things." (Yes, I promise you, she said that.) Then the situation grew worse due to the wrong correction to the mistake.

When the program began, one of the school leaders stood at the podium and said to everyone in that packed room, "It has come to my attention that one of the students who is receiving the Presidential Scholar's Award was not listed in your program. So if everyone could take a pen and write [and she gave his name] on your program, he can be added." My twelve-year-old son was humiliated. He was singled out and she had called him by his full name—including his middle name—

two things twelve-year-old boys abhor. It would have been better if she had simply called him across the stage at the appropriate time to receive the award without mentioning the error. This example teaches an important lesson: correct the error, if possible, and make sure it's the right corrective action for the situation.

- *Do your best to avoid making the same mistake twice.* One of the ways we recover from a mistake is to learn from it and not make the same mistake again. Early in my business career, I made a printing error. I produced a brochure for my company, and after it was printed I realized I had misspelled the word *restaurant.* This was especially inappropriate since I worked for a restaurant company, and I had been a journalism major in college! Now, every time I type that word, I double-check to see that it is spelled correctly. I have never made that mistake again. I often tell that story to my team members at work when they make a mistake. I want them to know I recognize that I make mistakes too, and that what I expect from them is to not make the same mistake twice.

  Unfortunately, there have been a few times I have made the same mistake twice. When that happens with one of my responsibilities at home, my husband and I discuss whether a certain task is my real talent. He is much more detail-oriented than me. He is meticulous about research, whether it is about a vacation we plan to take or a home appliance we need to purchase. I tend to be strategic, visionary, and creative. We have discovered that sometimes I move too fast and don't slow down for the details. Now when we are considering a big purchase, I tell him my ideas and what I think I want and he does the research to make sure we make the right decision. We realize that this works better for us.

We can recover from our mistakes if we own our mistakes and then apologize sincerely, correct them promptly, and avoid making the same mistakes twice. Most importantly, we cannot be paralyzed by our mistakes. Once we have taken these three actions, we need to let them go and move on, knowing we have done our best to resolve the situations.

Manage Your Diversity

Understanding the differences you bring to an organization and a team and how to leverage those differences will be important to keeping a job and growing a career. Leaders desire teams with strong chemistry; however, that does not mean they want to select talent that all think and look alike. The best leaders know that great team chemistry is created when the members think and act differently but are able to collaborate and find common ground. Doing so ensures success.

Some diversity is obvious, and some is not. Finding a way to effectively communicate your point of view while valuing the perspective of others is critical to your success. It is a delicate balance between fitting in and bringing your highest value to the team, which is your own unique perspective.

The best career advice I ever received was delivered in a very unexpected way by one of my leaders early in my career. I well remember the day he walked over to my desk and said, "You are young, and you are a female. Now get over it and win them over with your competence." With time, as I grew older, the first part of that statement took care of itself. In time, I learned to manage the second part of the statement. Too young to know it at the time, I did not fully understand the path in front of me, nor did I know how important it would be for me to remain undistracted by what I could not change. In time, I learned the importance of controlling what only I could control and letting go of the rest.

Three decades ago, the business world was a different place for women. I was extremely fortunate to work for an organization in which I felt valued, honored, and respected. At the time, there were not very many women in leadership, but I am grateful that several men took time to mentor me, sponsor me, and help me navigate a path toward leadership. Eventually, those men recognized my leadership capabilities, and I became the first female officer at my company. Did they always understand my unique perspective? No, nor could they, no more than I could always understand theirs. But I didn't focus on that. I took the advice from my earlier boss and focused on winning them over with my competence.

It's difficult when you are the "only one." Often, my perspective was very different, and it was challenging to find just the right way to offer my point of view. I was constantly trying to find the right balance between the perception of being too meek and too aggressive.

Instead of concerning myself with whether I was understood, I tried harder to understand. Instead of being sure my voice rose above others, I made sure my ears were listening to other voices. Instead of making everything a matter of the heart, I pushed myself to find the heart of the matter. Did I do this perfectly? Absolutely not. I messed up more times than I can count. There were times when I was too emotional for the circumstances, and other times when, exhausted from trying to find a way into a conversation, I gave up. Early in my career I was not a good listener but was constantly thinking about what I was going to say next. At other times, I was not competitive enough and was too quick to concede rather than stay in the debate.

Over the years, I benefited from wise counselors, coaches, and friends who are women. But because I lacked a female guide early in my career, it was important to me as my career grew to help other women navigate their paths. If I were coaching a younger me on how to manage my diversity in business, these are the six things I would suggest:

- *Seek first to understand and then to be understood.* You read this earlier in this book. Stephen Covey's fifth habit is my collaboration go-to thought. Listen before speaking. Ask clarifying questions. Be sure others feel heard. The process might change your thinking altogether, but at the very least, hopefully it will earn you the right to state your case or express your opinion.

- *Be yourself.* There are many great leaders to emulate, but you are likely in your role because of who you are. Don't try to be someone else. Bring the best of you into your work. Learn from others, and then be confident in yourself.

- *Don't make it personal.* The saying "It's not personal; it's business" might be true, or it might very well be personal. But you don't have to play along. Take the high road every time. Making it personal distracts you from everything you are trying to accomplish.

- *Pursue respect, not popularity.* A different boss early in my career told me, "It's more important to be respected than to be liked." Often, people who are respected are also well-liked, but don't get these out of order. Respect is earned by managing emotions and leading from competency.

- *Be willing to take risks.* It takes courage to bring our true selves into the team and share a different point of view. The best leaders will value it and encourage you to do so. The worst ones will overlook you and find themselves mired in groupthink. However, you simply cannot move forward in your career without taking some risks.

- *Help each other.* Have an abundance mentality about success with your fellow colleagues, male or female. There is enough opportunity for everyone, and someone else's success does not diminish your own. When you take a step up or forward, reach back and give a hand to someone else and bring them along.

I cannot guarantee or even suggest that in following this advice you will always be treated respectfully and appropriately. But what

I do know is this: you will feel strong. Just as it takes months and even years of consistent healthy habits to make our bodies strong, it takes the same kind of work to be strong in our professional lives.

Every morning, I get on my bike to strengthen muscles, bones, and organs. I must also practice principles that make me strong when I walk into my professional world. When we manage ourselves in such a way that we respect the person we see in the mirror, we are strong and are truly winning. When the organization embraces the best of every person on the team, they win too.

Respond to an Abusive Boss

If you work long enough, chances are you will at some time encounter an abusive boss in the workplace. It's disheartening, and it is truly one of the most challenging situations to manage. Many people simply leave the organization rather than confront it. But as that is not an option for everyone, and since there are difficult people everywhere, it is wise to learn how to handle these situations.

> "He refuses to collaborate!" Ellen was so frustrated with her boss. Even though Ellen was a tenured leader with a successful track record, her boss still felt it necessary to micromanage her work and even her team. Just as or more difficult, he was verbally and emotionally abusive to her and others. When she went on vacation or traveled for business, he took advantage of the opportunity to undermine her leadership. Showing up unannounced to meetings, berating the efforts of team members, and criticizing Ellen to others were common to his style.
>
> Ellen was stuck. It was a miserable experience for everyone to endure the tirades and shifting moods of her boss. However, like many bullies, he did an excellent job of managing up. Many who were not under his leadership saw him as a great strategist, mentor, and developer of people.

He was rapidly ascending the organization and seemed destined to soon sit on the organization's senior leadership team.

On her team, fear was the most prevalent emotion. She knew that if she did not correct the situation, the fear that enveloped her would soon impact her performance and her own ability to lead.

She sat across the table from her executive coach at a coffee shop, telling her story. In her long career, she had, fortunately, never encountered someone so difficult. What options should she consider? She had always loved her work and her organization, but she wasn't sleeping well and felt sick to her stomach every morning on the commute to work. She was tempted to leave, but she had too much invested to just walk away. Beyond that, she truly cared about the people on her team. But she had hit a wall and could not find a way forward. What could she do?

Ellen worked with her coach to create a plan to better manage her boss. Avoiding him and pretending not to be fazed by his actions had proven both unproductive and ineffective. Her coach suggested that she attempt to understand why her boss behaved the way he did. Was he genuinely dissatisfied with performance and inept at communicating it, or did his own insecurities dictate that he intimidate his staff into compliance? To get the answer, she would have to be willing to engage with her unpredictable, moody, and abusive boss.

With great courage, Ellen sat down in a one-on-one meeting with her boss and asked about his observations of her and the team. When it was evident he could not produce a viable concern, she attempted to set boundaries. Her first request was collaboration in setting strategy and assigning tasks for the team. Her boss quickly refused, stating that collaborating with her was not necessary and a waste of time. She had attempted the first important step in managing a bully—standing up to his behavior and setting boundaries.

Sometimes that is enough to change the pattern and relationship, but unfortunately, in this case it was not.

Finding herself at the crossroads of either resigning or resolving the situation, Ellen knew she had to reach out for help within the organization. Her boss's behavior was not in keeping with the organization's stated purpose, mission, and values, and she could not allow her team to be abused. It was her responsibility to deal with the situation for her sake and theirs.

Ellen, a very senior leader, met regularly with several C-suite leaders in the company, including the one in her chain of command. It was time to talk to her boss's boss. In each encounter with her boss, Ellen took very careful notes, either during the discussion or immediately afterward. To prepare for the upcoming meeting, Ellen carefully documented the instances of abuse, including the date, people present, words spoken, and exact behavior and actions of her boss. Her clear documentation revealed a pattern of behavior. Her documentation also served notice to the organization as to the severity of the situation.

As she had hoped, the C-suite leader listened to her concerns, conducted his own investigation, and took appropriate action by changing the responsibilities of Ellen's leader. What could have been a cultural disaster for the organization was resolved, the team was preserved, and the people on it were retained. Of course, every story does not end that well.

Should you find yourself in a similar situation, following are some steps to make your way forward:

- *Don't panic or succumb to fear.* Fear shuts us down, and we become incapable of making good decisions and taking appropriate action. Bullies count on that reaction. Be courageous and rise above the fear, and choose to respond instead of react.

- *Document carefully the setting, the behaviors, and the words.* At some point, you will need to share your observations with the bully or someone else, and you want to be sure you are able to clearly communicate the situation. Retain your documentation in a confidential location.

- *Seek counsel and avoid isolation.* Find someone trustworthy to talk to—a mentor, advisor, or coach—who can help you navigate resolution and keep you from feeling isolated. Isolation is a tool of bullies, and you want to eliminate it from his toolbox.

- *Stand up to the bully.* This advice goes all the way back to the primary school playground, but it is true in career situations too. Bullies attack people they think will not fight back. Set your boundaries and make it clear that, regardless of the consequences, you will not be treated that way. Every person deserves respect.

- *Report the issue to leadership.* If it is your leader who is being abusive, find another leader you trust to talk to or someone in your human resources or talent function departments. Most organizations understand the seriousness of workplace bullying, if only from a liability perspective. Organizations with healthy, strong cultures know that one bully can undermine the culture quickly and spread toxicity in the environment. If you state your well-documented case and do not find someone within the organization to help you, then it's time to leave. It's not the culture for you, and it could be detrimental to your overall well-being.

If organizations insist that everyone be treated with respect and hold leaders and others accountable for doing so, they can avoid situations like Ellen's. Remarkable cultures value the contributions of everyone and steward and sustain their talent. If you don't work for an organization like that, then find one or create your own.

Manage Your Ego

Nothing can hinder a career faster than the inability to manage our own egos. It takes skill to do it effectively. There is a delicate balance between effectively sharing your accomplishments and overly bragging.

When possible, communicate accomplishments as what "we" achieved rather than what "I" achieved. Few things are ever the result of our own singular effort. A wise leader is willing to share the credit and acknowledge and recognize other team members for their roles in successes. Being a strong contributor on a winning team is good for your career too!

Make others, not yourself, the heroes of your stories. Allow someone else to elevate you for your performance while you focus on supporting and encouraging others for theirs.

Avoid name-dropping with your coworkers. If you were fortunate enough to be invited to breakfast with the CEO, keep it to yourself. Your coworkers will not be offended by the fact that you had breakfast with the CEO, but they will be offended by your need to tell them about it.

> Bryan enjoyed being "in the know" and was a proficient name-dropper. Given the opportunity, he liked to share with others about his interactions with influential people in and out of the organization. In team meetings, he often wove into the conversation the special project he was working on for a company leader. It seemed as if he strategized about how he could place himself in opportunities to engage with senior leadership.
>
> The more visibility and special treatment Bryan received, the larger his ego grew. Regardless of the coaching he received, he could not stop himself from talking about his relationships with senior leaders. As social media evolved, he often shared photos of himself with influential people. An out-of-control ego was driving his choices. His

behavior was off-putting to his team and peers, and it dam-aged trust with his leader.

Eventually, his ego prevented him from advancing his career. Because he lacked self-awareness, Bryan did not realize that others believed him to be capable, competent, and talented. He did not need to expound on his accom-plishments and tout his influential relationships. Under-neath his ego was a man with a good heart, who worked hard and cared deeply for others. Unfortunately, his in-securities prevented him from managing his ego, and that eventually limited his career and destroyed relationships along the way.

The skills you acquire in learning to navigate the land mines you can see will also help you navigate the ones that sneak up on you. Ideally, we are prepared for every possible scenario, but that is neither realistic nor possible. Instead, we continue to learn les-sons from our experiences to help us make better decisions and grow a career over time.

WHAT'S MY STORY?

1. How do I currently manage rejection? What mindset shifts can I make to be more resilient?

2. Am I allowing myself to learn from mistakes, or do I con-stantly beat myself up for errors? How can I more posi-tively use mistakes as learning opportunities?

3. In group settings, am I holding back my perspective be-cause I feel different? Or am I expressing my perspective because I know that I offer a different point of view?

4. Do I use my differences to contribute to a team per-spective, or do I allow my differences to disrupt team chemistry?

5. Is there someone I need to stand up to who is not treating me with respect? What steps do I need to take to resolve the relationship?

6. Is my ego in check? Which behaviors do I need to correct to be sure that I am presenting myself as a collaborative team player and am not focused only on myself?

GROW A CAREER

PART III

Finding a job and keeping a job are just the beginning of navigating the path to making a living. Growing a career that provides for your needs and fulfills your dreams is usually a lifelong journey. Building networks, forming deep relationships, and developing yourself are critical milestones to growing a career. Hopefully, you will find people along the way eager to help you. Mostly, however, it is a "do it yourself" world. Regardless of the mentors and development programs available to you, your growth is largely dependent on your own personal investment.

Commit to lifelong learning. You may have obtained various undergraduate- and graduate-level degrees, but those academic opportunities did not teach you everything you need to know to be successful. The most valuable skill you obtained from your educational experiences is knowing how to learn, and you will need to use that skill the rest of your life. Use it to help you achieve your career dreams. How can you apply the skill of knowing how to learn? Consider reducing time scrolling social media and read books instead. View online training and developmental content and spend less time bingeing on Netflix. Exchange some online video-game time for conversations with leaders.

Establish habits that will help you grow and learn throughout your career. Practice those habits from the very beginning. Motivational speaker Charlie "Tremendous" Jones often said, "You will be the same person five years from now except for the people you meet and the books that you read."[1] Read the books, meet the people, and watch how you learn and grow. Employees who consistently learn new skills are more valuable and enjoy more success. The relationships you develop and the capabilities you obtain from the pursuit of lifelong learning will prepare you to be successful in every role and opportunity of your career.

8

Developing Yourself

My young client, Thad, sat across the table from me, expressing doubts about everything from his current company to his career choice. All I could see was opportunity, while all he could see was uncertainty.

What was clear to me but not as obvious to Thad was that he had not decided to go all in. He was just going through the motions to be good enough, not the best he could be. He had dipped his toes in the water, sometimes wading into the shallow end, but he had not taken the plunge into the deep end in order to fully commit to the investment of developing himself.

The term *all in* is probably way overused these days, but it helps to explain what was hindering my coaching client's progress. Thad carefully calculated the effort required to meet the minimal expectations for his role. What he was missing was a commitment to make the necessary sacrifices and even the vulnerability to be all in for his own success.

After our meeting, I assessed our conversation and reflected on why he was holding back. I came to the conclusion that he was unsure the effort would be worth the outcome. Recognizing that his company was likely to be sold within twenty-four months, he was unsure of his future. This was shortsighted on his part because he was failing to recognize that whatever he invested in his current role would better prepare him for his next one.

Thad only saw uncertainty, which caused him to reluctantly withhold the very thing he needed to do to be successful: give 100 percent of his effort. If his mindset had been one of opportunity, he would have been willing to do whatever was necessary to make himself successful in his present opportunity or one he might have in the future.

Intelligence, physical ability, and talent are certainly factors that contribute to success, but one of the biggest keys to success is determining to be all in on your career, including your development. It's the intersection where attitude trumps aptitude.

Find a Mentor

Within some organizations, mentors are assigned. That may or may not be the best opportunity for you. It really depends on how skilled they are at mentoring others. It also depends on how committed they are to helping you grow. If it is only an assigned part of their job, they may not be very dedicated to helping you. I have found that the best mentors are the ones we choose ourselves who are not only willing to assist but also very enthusiastic about helping us grow.

Over the course of my career, I have had several mentors, but not all of them were effective in the role. This appears to be a common theme, so it is important to choose mentors carefully. Riley, who shared his story with me, said that his mentor spent two hours each month with him. He used most of that time to talk negatively about other people and gauge Riley's reaction. Riley was exhausted after every session with him. He did mention one positive outcome: he learned how to pivot conversations and turn negativity into positivity during his time with the mentor. If we are open to it, there is something to learn from every opportunity, even the ones that are primarily negative.

Casey, another individual who shared her story with me, was disappointed with her mentor. She said he was great at giving her advice, but he never invited her into his world of work. She would have benefited from watching him in action as he negotiated business deals and interacted with senior leaders. While he gave great advice sitting across the lunch table, she would have learned much more had he engaged her more in his role. Successful mentors give their mentees an inside look at their thinking, experiences, and day-to-day activities.

Often, the best mentor is from outside your organization and can be from a different industry or generation. An outside viewpoint is often the most valuable perspective.[1] Choosing someone from a different organization allows for unbiased input and opens the door for you to be more forthright in the conversation. The downside of that choice is that sometimes they do not understand the culture you are trying to navigate. On the other hand, they are focused only on coaching your responses without regard to the personalities and behaviors of others. Such advisement helps you focus on what you can control and let go of what you cannot control.

The ability to meet face-to-face with a mentor is ideal. However, it is often difficult to find someone who can give you one-on-one coaching. Usually, the people you are looking for have time constraints that limit their availability, regardless of how much they would like to help. The demand for great mentors far exceeds the supply.[2] Even so, you can find a mentor if you are willing to invest the effort in your own development. Following are some steps you can take:

- *Establish your own goals and expectations.* Be sure you know what you want to accomplish with a mentor. What skills do you hope to develop? What behaviors do you want to change?

What competencies do you wish to learn? Answering these questions will assist you in communicating your goals to your mentor and help you to identify the right mentor.

- *Join networking groups that will connect you with mentor candidates.* Attend the meetings and functions for people who share your interests and experiences. Invest the time to talk with others and establish meaningful connections. Look for online groups within sites such as LinkedIn that are opportunities to connect with potential mentors. Ask former professors and internship supervisors for the names of those they know in the industry who might be able to help you.

- *Agree with the mentor as to how often and how long you will meet.* Then be prepared with an agenda for each meeting. Send the agenda to your mentor ahead of time so you both can be thinking about how to add value to your time together.

- *Respect the mentor's time.* Never extend the time beyond that allotted unless invited to do so by your mentor. Stay on the topic, and don't get distracted with other subjects. Take advantage of every opportunity to learn. If your mentor suggests you attend one of their meetings or speaking engagements, try to make yourself available. This communicates that you are grateful for the help and that you respect their time and interest in you.

- *Look beyond personal interactions for mentoring.* Blogs, podcasts, books, courses, conferences, online videos, and membership sites all offer opportunities to learn from the experts. You may not be able to get Bob Goff or Brené Brown to be your mentor, but you can certainly learn from other sources much of what they would tell you in a one-on-one engagement.

- *Be grateful.* Go out of your way to demonstrate gratitude to your mentor. Their most valuable commodity is time. Show you're grateful for the time your mentor has given to you.

Send handwritten notes, buy a Christmas gift, or pick up
a lunch tab. These are small acts that demonstrate you are
invested in your own development and grateful to have their
help.

Ashley graduated from college in 2014 and is now a product manager at DaySpring. She sought out a mentor while
still in college, which helped to prepare her to land a job
upon graduation. Ashley says:

During my time in college, I met my mentor through
the person who was my boss at the time. Mr. Wright was a
businessman and a trustee at the university. As I interacted
with him, I discovered he was full of wisdom from his life
and work experience. I not only learned from him, but it
was also fun to listen to his stories and experiences. A few
weeks after running into him numerous times on campus,
I asked him to consider being my mentor. He said he was
honored by the request and said yes.

As I was mentored by Mr. Wright, he helped me think
about jobs to apply for and what marketplace realities
I would face upon graduation. He helped set a realistic
expectation on compensation and what entry-level job responsibilities would entail. At his suggestion, I took numerous personality assessments. We talked through those, and
it helped me understand how my strengths could be beneficial in a job. He also gave me feedback about what might
hinder me and how to manage myself within an organization.

During my senior year, I was part of the Leadership Fel-
lows program at my college, which was started by my mentor. The program paired groups of students with local mentors who were leaders in the community. The ongoing
mentorship program helped prepare me for my future job.

Applying for jobs during my senior year was a little
more difficult than I expected. I thought I would be an easy
hire, but after a few rejections, I became a little discouraged. During this process, my mentor was invaluable. He

continued to remind me that I was a great candidate, but that I was fresh out of college and needed to get some experience. Mr. Wright encouraged me to be patient and to believe that the right opportunity would soon present itself. He was also very helpful in explaining how things work in a corporate environment and that sometimes the selection process can take longer than we expect. Thankfully, about a month before graduation, I heard back from a corporation and received a job offer. It was the beginning of a great career so far.

I am forever grateful for my mentor and still interact with him from time to time. In fact, I just invited him and his wife to my wedding festivities. My one piece of advice for anyone desiring a mentor, whether while still in college or in the job market, is to ask someone to be your mentor. Do not wait for them to find you as that likely will not happen. If you meet someone who has more life experience than you do and appears to enjoy teaching and coaching others, simply ask if he or she would consider being your mentor. The worst thing that can happen is that they say no, and then you just find someone else to ask!

Volunteer

Volunteer service contributes more to growing our careers than an added category to the résumé. The real value of volunteering is learning new skills and building new relationships. Of the skills we gain by volunteering, perhaps the most important one is learning to serve others. Knowing how to serve and the principles of service helps us grow our careers.

The skills we gain by volunteering are transferrable and are necessary to growing any career.[3] By volunteering, we learn interpersonal skills, delegation, time management, listening, problem solving, customer service, and teamwork. Volunteer work gives us the opportunity to learn and apply skills we may not have yet used on the job. Often, it is volunteer work that provides the first opportunity to lead people or lead a project.

During my career, one of the ways I volunteered outside of work was through mission work in Kenya. There were many skills that I honed both stateside and on the ground in Kenya. I worked with teams of people from diverse backgrounds and spanning several age groups. These situations helped develop my interpersonal skills. Due to the cultural differences, language barriers, and technology challenges, the mission field was a great place to develop my problem-solving skills.

On one particular two-week trip, I was leading a group of women. I was already feeling hesitant about the trip because of terrorist threat warnings that had been issued in Kenya. While the threat of terrorism is always present, in this case, the British government had asked their citizens to refrain from going to Kenya, believing they had intelligence to suggest an imminent terrorist attack.

When our group arrived at the Atlanta airport for departure to Amsterdam with a connection to Nairobi, our flight was delayed due to a mechanical problem. For several days beforehand, I had contemplated canceling the trip due to the travel warnings, and the longer the flight was delayed, the more my concerns intensified. I wondered if it was an indication that we should stay home.

After checking with the gate agent about travel options, I gathered the team so that we could make a decision together. One option was to wait for this flight, which would likely leave many hours later, causing us to miss our connection and requiring an overnight stay in Amsterdam before going on to Nairobi. Alternatively, we could go home and try to get a different flight to Nairobi the next day.

After much conversation, we decided to wait for our flight to Amsterdam and spend a night there before continuing to Nairobi on a different flight. I handled all the ticket exchanges with the airline and then sent messages to our hosts in Africa. In my heart, I believed we would get to Amsterdam and the trip to Kenya would be canceled due to the security threats. I was already imagining what alternative plans we could make for our unexpected stay in Europe.

Finally, we boarded our overnight flight to Amsterdam. We arrived there mid-afternoon, and the airline provided us with hotel rooms for the night. However, I still had to get a group of fifteen people from the airport to the hotel in a cost-effective way. The Netherlands did not have ride-share apps at that time. I organized taxis and transported the team.

We were tired and went to our rooms. I just wanted a shower and a night's rest in a bed before continuing our journey, but first I turned on the TV to the BBC channel to see what was happening in the world. The BBC were begging British citizens not to go to Kenya due to an "imminent terrorist attack." We had a tough decision to make the next morning.

Having promised the team I would share any security information with them, I arrived at breakfast, told them what I had seen on the news, and asked them what they wanted to do. They said, "Let's go to the airport." They believed, and I concurred, that if we were not supposed to go, the group would not get through security, the flight would be canceled, or some other obstacle would be placed in our way.

Getting through international security turned out to be easier than with any group I had ever led. We had no problems, and for the most part, that is the way the entire trip unfolded. Sadly, the "imminent" attack took place eighteen months later when a popular shopping mall in Nairobi was taken over by terrorists, and seventy-one people lost their lives in a mass shooting.

In the fourteen days I led that team, I learned skills that sometimes take years to learn on the job. Navigating delays, calming team members' fears, making decisions that impact the lives of others, communicating effectively with a team, and managing changes in itinerary and logistics were a few of the skills that I learned and honed on that trip. Volunteering is an excellent way to grow skills that will serve you well in your work role and in future roles.

Look for opportunities in your community, your company, your professional networks, your former fraternity or sorority, and your church and local parachurch organizations. Choose an organization for which you have a lot of passion and that offers opportunities to grow the skills you need to strengthen. Most companies today offer time for employees to serve either organizations the company supports or an organization of employees' choosing.

Occasionally, a volunteer role becomes a career. For Justin Miller, serving others is a value that was instilled in him early in life. His dad, Mark, often said to him, "There's a real world out there, and we are not living in it." To help Justin understand the world better, his dad provided opportunities for him to voluntarily serve in his community and globally. Justin describes volunteerism as part of his family culture. When he was younger, he did not envision his volunteer work leading him into his career. Volunteerism was a way to give back in thankfulness for the blessings in his life.[4]

All of that changed early in college. Justin attended the Global Leadership Summit in 2006 and listened to a message by music artist Bono. Justin was moved by the statistics Bono shared, including that twenty-five million people from sub-Saharan Africa were living with HIV/AIDS.[5] He went on to say that people were dying from the disease at an alarming rate: sixty-five hundred Africans each day.[6] Then Bono made a statement that stirred Justin's soul: "Everyone in the world was trying to work together to see progress in the areas, and the church not being a part of it was unacceptable. It wouldn't be acceptable in history and it wouldn't be acceptable to God."[7]

Before he knew it, the college sophomore and two of his best friends were on their way to Kenya for the purpose of making a documentary to show to churches with the hope of engaging both their hearts and their treasure in response to the AIDS crisis in Africa. The young men were fortunate to be connected to the right people and able to turn their vision into reality, and their fundraising efforts provided the cash they needed for the project. What they witnessed in Kenya in 2006 and included in their documentary changed their lives. Though Justin did not know it at the time, his calling was already turning into a career.

The pastors they met in Kenya shared a proposal with Justin to care for an underserved and vulnerable population: parents with HIV. They wanted to preserve families and prevent orphans by providing medical and nutritional support, counseling, and job skills training to parents and caregivers living with HIV. While still in college, Justin put the wheels in motion to fund and serve CARE for AIDS, partnering with churches in Kenya and raising money from churches in the United States.

Upon graduation from Vanderbilt University, Justin had plenty of opportunities to pursue a career in the for-profit corporate world, but his lifelong volunteerism experiences had led him to a different path, and he made the decision to go all in and lead the CARE for AIDS organization. Since 2007, CARE for AIDS has opened sixty-eight centers in Kenya, Uganda, and Tanzania, and over seventeen thousand clients have completed their programs. More than two hundred people are employed in Africa and the United States by the ministry.[8]

Justin credits his volunteer experience with teaching him some important leadership skills. He learned how to cast and communicate a vision to donors, potential team members, board members, and volunteers. He learned how to tell stories that motivate people to join the effort. He also learned how to build a business case to show return on investment and to sell a concept with no tangible results yet in place. Above everything else, Justin said that volunteering helped him be a better problem solver. Volunteers are often thrust into a group of diverse people and asked to deliver a service, complete a project, raise money, or solve a problem.

Leading volunteers strengthens people skills too. Justin said that learning to motivate people with extrinsic rewards is hard enough; motivating people by intrinsic value is even more difficult. Skill development through volunteerism is not limited to just hard skills either. Volunteering can increase empathy, emotional intelligence, and awareness of others and their circumstances.

Today, Justin selects talent for his organization and carefully evaluates their volunteer experience. He is looking for people driven by a passion to serve, not those just desiring to fill a résumé with community service hours. He says he looks for people who are givers rather than takers and who are compelled to make a difference in the world through their own personal mission.

If you are looking for ways to grow skills you are not currently using at work, seek opportunities to volunteer. Find one whose purpose matches your own and for which you sense a calling. Before long, you will likely transfer the skills you gain volunteering to your role at work.

Serve on Boards

Serving on nonprofit boards is another excellent way to develop yourself outside of your job. It offers the same benefits as volunteering, but also allows you to participate in decision making for an organization. Board membership provides the opportunity to advise the leadership of the organization in setting strategic direction and managing financial health and to engage with other leaders to achieve shared vision and goals.

Joining a board can also enhance your career, particularly if you have spent most of it in one function. Board membership offers a high-level understanding of an organization and exposure to other disciplines. While I was often asked to join boards because of my human-resources expertise, I enjoyed using other capabilities such as writing, communicating, and marketing.

For some people, board service is their first leadership opportunity. Because boards can have a number of subcommittees, almost every board member gains leadership experience while serving. In addition to leading a committee, there can be opportunities to mentor new members who join the board.

Strengthening your professional network is another benefit of serving on a board. You are able to develop relationships with others across industries, and those connections may lead to your next opportunity. If you manage your board position well and contribute to the success of the organization, you will also increase your professional credibility and reputation.

Throughout my career, I served on a number of boards and chaired three of them. At the time I served on one of the boards, I was the only female director on it. Quarterly, I sat at the head of a long mahogany table surrounded by men sitting in high leather-back chairs. It was the perfect experience for me to lead that board because it was similar to the situation and demographic in my current job. I was the only woman in the room there too!

The board-chair assignment helped me work on my skills of communicating and collaborating with an all-male team in a non-threatening way. When I presided over board meetings, I was always astounded that they listened to me and supported my ideas and suggestions. If only it was so easy in the corporate world!

Many nonprofits need and are searching for leaders, emerging leaders, and future leaders to serve on their boards and provide governance for their organizations. Your organization might even hold a standing seat on a local board to provide developmental opportunities for their emerging leaders.

Nonprofit organizations often invite people who are volunteering in the organization to serve on the board. If you receive such an invitation, interview the leader and other board members about their experiences. Ask to attend a board meeting to see how the board functions and whether you believe you will be able to contribute successfully.

Respond to Change

Years ago, a work colleague of mine often said, "Change is my friend, and I will embrace it." I was young in my career and had no understanding of the value of that statement. When faced with change, especially unexpected change, our first response is often to react or resist instead of to respond.

Eighteen months into my first job, my boss unexpectedly resigned. It was particularly unusual because it was uncommon for people to leave the company, especially at senior levels of the organization. While I selected the company as the place I wanted to work, I had also chosen to work for him. I responded poorly to the change. I was emotional and focused only on me. I was overconcerned with what was going to happen to me instead of focusing on the needs of everyone on the team impacted by his sudden departure. His departure eventually set me up for an incredible career-growth opportunity, but I lacked vision to see it at the time because I was reacting to and resisting the change. I was quite fortunate that my behavior did not have a negative impact on my career.

Developing ourselves requires us to manage and navigate change. Change is inevitable, and the question we must ask ourselves when faced with change is, Do I react or do I respond to change? The answer will determine if we grow in seasons of change or if we get stuck. Candidly, I was an expert at reacting when I was younger. If I could go back and give my younger self advice about how to positively respond to change, this is what I would tell her:

- *Be still.* That may sound like an odd first step to managing change. The first response to change is not to do but to think. Think it through and look at all sides. Seek to understand the change. Process the change through your mind and through your heart. Identify what you are feeling about it: grief, anger, excitement, challenge, fear, and so on. Naming the emotion helps us to respond, not react or resist.

- *Envision a response.* How we respond to change impacts our credibility with others who are observing our behavior, including the boss and other teammates. Give lots of thought as to how a response or reaction will impact those around you. Our response can help the team move forward or cause the team to stagnate.

- *Process with a trusted advisor.* Talking to a spouse, best friend, counselor, coach, or mentor brings the response plan to life and allows us to process thoughts, feelings, and ideas in a safe environment. It is important to seek transparent and truthful feedback from someone who is "for" us. A trusted advisor can offer a different perspective and help us refine our response plan.

- *Embrace change.* Once we have identified the feelings surrounding significant change, it is time to move forward. The timetable varies, depending on the type of change. In general, recovering from grief takes longer to adjust to, but in all cases, at some point, we must move forward.

- *Be game ready.* I am not suggesting that we should not be our authentic selves, but we need to be ready to play if we step onto the field. One of my trusted advisors taught me this: *If I can't play, I don't stay.* For me to give my best to the team and our shared goals, I must show up ready to support and contribute in all circumstances, even during significant change. If not, I drain energy from the entire team and put our success at jeopardy.

- *Seize the opportunity.* There is opportunity in every change. My husband and I went through an intense period of change that included losing our parents and empty nesting at the same time. But even in losing our parents, we paused to think about the things we wanted to do together, the places we wanted to travel, and the importance of putting our own "house in order." With changes at work, there is always something new to be learned, new achievements possible, and a different impact to make. When our son married, it changed our relationship, as it should, but we gained a daughter and we have two new adult friends in our lives.

- *Continue to seek feedback.* Ask others to help you understand how you are responding to and impacting others during times of great change. When we respond rather than react, we have a greater chance of positive influence. Feedback is critical to helping us navigate change and evaluate our response to the change.

- *Prepare for more change.* Change is constant throughout our lives, and if we can learn through each cycle, we are better prepared to respond and not react to change when the next cycle surfaces. Responding, not reacting, can become ingrained in our habits and soon become core to who we are.

When we refuse to change, we are done. If we don't want to be done in any arena of life, including work, we must embrace change, respond, and grow.

Fortunately, the organization found a suitable role for me after my boss resigned. In fact, his resignation provided opportunities for me to immediately grow my career. I could not see it at the time, as is often the case when we encounter change. To grow a successful career, we must recognize that change will occur frequently and early on develop the skills to navigate change.

Craft an "Elevator Speech"

You have seen it in the movies or perhaps even lived it in your job. A young associate is on the elevator at the office. As she is scrolling through her phone, riding to her floor, the doors open and someone joins her. She finally looks up and realizes she is on the elevator with one of the C-suite members of the organization. In this brief one-minute-or-less ride on the elevator, she has the opportunity for visibility with one of the most senior members of her company. When he says "What's up?" the only words to come out of her mouth are "Not much."

At some point, you will get on the elevator and there will be a member of senior leadership in the company riding with you. You will have about sixty seconds to leave a meaningful impression. They will ask you how it's going. You want to say something besides "great." Be prepared to share one thing you are working on and how it's helping the company. Your answer might sound like this: "I just finished preparing the rollout for XYZ technology, and I think it will make our response to customers much faster." You may want to say something that leaves the door open for future conversation, such as "I am on my way to Omaha to meet with a potential client who is really interested in our distribution capability. I will let you know how it goes." These responses will make a strong impression, and the leader in the elevator might remember you when new opportunities arise. Of course, change up your answer to match something you are currently managing. In the days of working virtually, this exchange might be over a Zoom call or on Slack, but the principles of how to respond still apply.

In his book *The Ride of a Lifetime*, Bob Iger, former CEO of the Walt Disney Company, tells the story of unexpectedly finding himself in the men's room with Roone Arledge. Bob was very early in his career at ABC Sports, and Roone was head of ABC Sports. As Bob tells the story, he was surprised that Roone began talking to him. He asked Bob how it was going, and Bob responded, "Well, some days I feel like it's tough and I am just keeping my head above water." Roone responded, "Get a longer snorkel," and walked out of the restroom. Bob was unprepared for his opportunity, but fortunately for him, it had no long-term impact.[9]

In large and small companies, it is common to have limited opportunity to interact with senior leaders. When the opportunity presents itself, you need to be prepared. Create an infomercial about yourself and your work that could be shared on a sixty-second elevator ride or in a five-minute virtual coffee chat. Following are some tips on crafting your own "elevator speech" to be ready for any unexpected opportunity:

- *Introduce yourself and where you work in the organization if you have not previously met the leader.* Avoid introducing yourself by title, but instead, say what you actually do.
- *Be prepared to talk about one project or initiative on which you are currently working.* Share information that will elicit further inquiry about the project.
- *Share a specific result that has benefited the company.* As you share results, don't take all the credit; use the word *we* instead of *I.*
- *Mention how excited you are about a new company initiative.* It could be anything from an announcement on a new plant opening, a new product, a new marketing campaign, or the company's latest green initiative. The important thing is that you are aware of your company's activities and you exhibit genuine interest.

Taking advantage of this type of moment can provide you with valuable visibility in the organization and increase your opportunities for growth and more responsibility.

Pursue Role Changes and Job Rotations

During my tenured career at one organization, I had the "best of the best" leadership-development opportunities. I attended multiple executive-education courses at the top business schools in the United States. In that organization, no expense is spared for leadership development. Their program includes one-on-one coaching from some of the best leadership minds and constant exposure to top-leadership conferences and speakers. The organization ensures participation in multiple mentoring programs, assignments to nonprofit boards, and engagement in a multitude of on-the-job experiences with the most senior leaders in the company. While these leadership-development tactics have the potential to contribute to leadership growth, none of them compare to the one that transformed me as a leader.

For thirty years, I worked in the same function within the organization—Human Resources, later renamed Talent. On my thirtieth anniversary with the company, I left the familiar and launched a new function and team, Enterprise Social Responsibility, something I knew very little about at the time. With the new assignment came a blank sheet of paper to develop a strategy, a new team to lead whom I did not select, a new leader in an unfamiliar area of the company, and a charge to "figure it out." It was the single most effective leadership-development activity of my entire career. Since then, I have become an advocate for organizations to formally adopt leadership-rotation programs as part of their leadership-development plans.

Often, businesses and even nonprofits anticipate the pain of change to be greater than the value of learning, so they avoid leadership rotation, especially if things are going well. However, an organization cannot afford for their leaders and staff to become complacent and their learning to atrophy. While stability in tenured leadership at the highest levels of the organization creates some comfort for collaboration, it can adversely impact innovation. Furthermore, leaders who stay in a position too long can shift into an "automatic" mode in both strategic thinking and their people management. Soon, complacency develops.

Consider the following benefits of a leadership-rotation program:

- *Leaders learn the valuable skill of building trust with a team.* True leadership does not require leaders to have expertise in a specific subject matter. Instead, it requires them to lead people who do. Leaders who lack subject-matter competency must rely on the subject-matter experts on their team to provide information and help make the best decisions. Trust breeds trust. When leaders trust their team members, the team members often reciprocate. Trust is foundational to the success of any leader.

- *Leaders learn critical persuasion and negotiation skills.* It is easier to advocate for and negotiate about a very familiar function. It's much more challenging to do so in unfamiliar territory. Yet it is the discomfort of the unfamiliar that promotes growth in leaders. Significant challenge to thinking and planning skills helps a leader's competencies evolve.

- *Leaders are more likely to develop an innovation mindset.* If a leader stays in one function too long, it is more difficult to think about how to do things differently. Leadership rotation can reignite some of the ideation that is natural to leaders, which can move the organization forward to meet future challenges.

- *Leaders strengthen people-management skills.* In most cases, established leaders are selecting the talent for the team, and that talent is choosing to work for that leader. However, when a leader is reassigned to a team, when the leader did not select the team members and they did not select the leader, new skills in leading people are required. The leader will need to focus on communication skills, role definition, goal setting, holding others accountable, and performance management. All leaders with teams should be applying these skills, but doing so in a new environment with new team members accelerates leadership development.

- *Leaders develop collaboration skills.* When assigned to a new role, especially if the functional competencies are unfamiliar, leaders will grow not only trust with team members but also collaboration skills with peers. The new subject matter will require the leader to seek input, counsel, and feedback from other leaders in the organization. It's not business as usual. Interdependency develops within the leadership team when leaders are challenged by new roles.

Within tenured organizations, leadership development can be especially challenging. There are too few new activities or programs that disrupt the leader's thinking and perspective. If you are presented with an opportunity to participate in a job rotation or leadership rotation, it could transform your career.

An important part of self-development is choosing to spend your discretionary time wisely. Download books and development content for long flights. Keep something to read in your backpack or on your mobile device for those unexpected down moments. Look for online videos that speak to an area you are addressing in your own development. Set aside time each day dedicated to learning something new, even if it is only ten minutes. Over time, short periods of investing in yourself will add up and pay dividends to your development.

As you commit to being a lifelong learner, look for organizations that support your learning and development goals as you pursue different roles, jobs, and organizations. At the same time, take responsibility for your own development and growth by investing in yourself and using the resources available to you. Self-development is one of the worthiest investments we can make to help us grow our careers. See my list of recommended resources in the back of this book.

WHAT'S MY STORY?

1. In my current role, am I all in on pursuing my own development and in my commitment to my role? What mindsets and behaviors need to change?

2. Whom could I connect with to serve as my mentor? What goals do I want to achieve with a mentor? If I currently have a mentor, what can I do to make the investment more valuable?

3. Which of my skills can I use in volunteering? What skills could I develop further by volunteering? What organizations do I know of that are looking for volunteers?

4. Which of my skills could benefit a nonprofit board? What causes am I passionate enough about to invest hours supporting their board? Which skills would I like to develop further by serving on a board? Who is one person I can reach out to for assistance in finding a board role?

5. What major changes have I experienced at work? How have I managed those changes? What should I do differently if presented with similar situations? What changes can I anticipate and prepare for now?

6. Am I able to articulate in thirty seconds my role in the organization and the value I add? Who can listen to my "elevator speech" and provide feedback to me? Which leaders in my organization am I likely to interact with, and how can I prepare to engage with them if given the opportunity?

7. If I were to rotate from my current role, what type of position appeals to me? What skills do I need to strengthen to prepare me for a role I want? Who in the organization might sponsor me for a job rotation?

9

Leading Others

The bright morning sun overwhelmed my screened-in porch, and I watched as the ficus tree in the planter in the corner soaked in the warmth of the rays. I noticed how it had grown in recent weeks by stretching its branches and leaning toward the window to take advantage of both the sun and humidity. The infusion of sun and moisture had caused this beautiful plant to grow upward.

There is something so satisfying about seeing a living thing grow and be healthy, stretching out to absorb that which nurtures it. The image caused me to pause in my morning quiet time and ask myself a question: Am I growing up?

That may sound like a very silly question at my age. Of course, I am growing up, right? Not necessarily. We all grow older, but we don't all grow up.

Think back to when you were little and finished the familiar sentence, "When I grow up, I want to be . . ." I assume that most people, like me, completed that sentence with something they wanted to be rather than someone they wanted to become.

Choosing something to be and choosing someone to become are two very different things. "I want to be a firefighter" is very different from "I want to be a mature, wise, kind, and generous person."

Like the ficus tree on my porch, growing up requires us to stretch and yearn for the things that nurture us. If we stop growing up, we just grow old, and we'll begin to wither just like the plant would without sunlight and humidity.

If we have been called to lead others, it is imperative that we continually grow up, and it is quite obvious that the more we grow up, the better we will lead. What nurtures a leader to grow up? How can you grow as an emerging leader?

- *Envision the person you want to become.* True leaders don't focus on a title or a role; instead, they focus on the kind of person they need to be to lead well. They identify the character qualities they need and want to develop and accept that the titles and position will follow.

- *Nurture your soul.* Leaders focused on becoming the person they were destined to be will do the hard "soul work" of developing their self-image. Great leaders have self-awareness and self-confidence that come from a deep understanding of themselves.

- *Develop your mind.* Reading, studying, learning from other leaders, and taking on stretching assignments keep a leader's mind engaged and sharp.

- *Invest in others.* The old saying that you learn what you teach is true. Investing in others is certainly important to preparing the next generation of leaders, but it also gives leaders the opportunity to reflect on, repeat, and reinforce the principles they know to be true. This practice not only grows others but also grows leaders.

- *Take care of yourself.* If leaders completely deplete themselves of energy, they cannot be effective. An important skill of a leader is the ability to rest mind and body, allowing themselves to refresh and have more to give to those they lead. Leadership is a lifelong journey, and to go the distance, they must take care of their bodies, minds, and hearts. For all the drive, initiative, and ambition that fill a leader's day, there must be equal opportunity to play, relax, and rest. It creates the rhythm that allows them to go the distance.

Dwell for a little longer on whether you want to grow up or just grow old. If you want to grow up, consider how you can incorporate these five actions into your lifestyle. If you have drifted from your original vision, revisit those ideas. Growing up sounds like a much better option than simply growing old.

You may be given a chance to lead a project or a team of people early in your career. Sometimes, the leader is chosen because of strong performance in a contributor role but without much preparation to be a leader. The study of leadership goes far beyond the scope of growing a career, but there are some actions a new leader can take early in a new assignment to secure quick wins.

Inspire Others

Integrity is a cornerstone attribute of a great leader. If you have been chosen for leadership, you are likely already thought of as someone with integrity. Each leader's integrity is shaped by life lessons and experiences. Early in this book, I shared about my first lesson in integrity when I stole candy from the grocery store as a child. That experience shaped me. It taught me to do the right thing, even when it is hard. The lessons I learned about integrity at age five shaped my foundation as a leader.

If we want to inspire followership, we need to lead with integrity. Self-improvement author Napoleon Hill wrote, "Without a sense of fairness and justice, no leader can command and retain the respect of his followers."[1] Integrity is often the first quality followers evaluate in a new leader. When times are difficult, followers often decide whether to stay or leave based on the integrity of the leader. They ask themselves, Is this someone I can respect and trust?

What can you do early in your leadership assignment to inspire your team? Lead with integrity by doing the following five things:

- *Always tell the truth, even when it is hard.* Leaders with integrity are transparent and forthcoming with information. If employees do not know what is happening around them, they have the tendency to misunderstand or misread a leader's intentions and possibly think the worst. When a leader sugarcoats the truth or only tells employees what they want to hear, trust decreases and credibility is at risk.

- *Admit your mistakes.* Leaders with integrity allow themselves to be vulnerable and admit their shortcomings so that those around them can learn from their mistakes. Ask yourself, Do I exhibit clarity of intent? Do I operate with purity of motive? These are critical questions when striving to lead with integrity and inspire others.

- *Do what you say you will do.* Leaders with integrity walk the talk and keep their promises. They do what they say they will do, when they say they will do it, and how they say they will do it. They are accountable to their leaders, their teams, their clients, and other stakeholders to fulfill their commitments.

- *Demonstrate respect for others, authority, and resources.* Leaders with integrity treat everyone with honor, dignity, and respect, even those who they perceive are unable to do anything for them. They demonstrate respect by being good stewards of resources, both people and money.

- *Take the high road every chance you get, and stand up for what is right.* Leaders with integrity avoid highlighting the failures of others. They focus on their own opportunities and challenges. Great leaders pursue the highest good for those they serve and strive to find the win-win in all situations.

No one does this perfectly, but leaders with integrity who want to inspire others model these behaviors. This is an excellent list for emerging leaders who desire to prepare their character for future opportunities.

Move from Doing to Leading

Transitioning from doing to leading is one of the most difficult adjustments for a new leader. However, to grow a career and especially to be entrusted as a leader, it is critical to be adept at setting a strategy and implementing what's required to execute it. For many new leaders, it is difficult to let go of the day-to-day tactics of the work and focus on the bigger picture. It's the difference between a photo snapped in pano view and one taken in portrait view. The portrait view displays a beautiful elk in a meadow of flowers at the foot of a mountain blurred in the background. The panoramic photo reveals that the elk was in a meadow next to a large lake in the midst of an enormous snowcapped mountain range.

The role of the leader is to see the complete picture—to understand where the organization wants to go and to be able to formulate a tactical plan to get there. But often, a really good "doer" is promoted to a position of leadership without having developed the ability to strategize for the future. This results in a leader who is a great taskmaster, doing more and expecting their team to follow, but who doesn't achieve the ultimate goals of the function and the organization.

Psychologist and journalist Daniel Goleman, an expert on emotional intelligence, writes, "Pacesetting works well when all of the employees are self-motivated, highly competent and need little direction or coordination." But it also "destroys the climate, and many employees feel overwhelmed by the pacesetter's demands."[2]

This behavior can also lead to a burned-out leader and exhausted followers.

This was one of my biggest mistakes as an emerging leader. I loved my work as an individual contributor, and my personality and achievement orientation drove me to work very hard. With little preparation for my first supervisory responsibility, I assumed everyone on my team was wired like me and was willing to put in really long hours of hard work. Furthermore, I continued "doing" along with leading, and they struggled to keep up with the growing demands communicated by my work ethic.

I expected my team to join the vision and be as passionate as I was about our goals. I failed to notice that explaining only the why of our work was insufficient. Many of them needed to be taught the how as well. Without instruction, there was no way a team member could perform to my satisfaction, so I kept doing, believing no one could do it as well as me. I created a vicious cycle of failing to teach, expecting more, being disappointed, and then just doing it myself.

One day, I realized the culture I had created on my team. I was surrounded by talent, many of whom were smarter and more capable than me. However, my leadership style had hindered both their development and their contribution. I had to break the "doing" cycle and start effectively delegating so that I could lead the team.

To avoid failure in my first leadership opportunity, I had to quickly change my mindset. It is one of the most difficult shifts to make but absolutely necessary to grow a career. World-renowned leadership coach Marshall Goldsmith writes, "What got you here won't get you there."[3] The ideal time to make this shift is before being appointed to a leadership role. But sometimes, because of the tactical responsibilities, that is impractical. Following are some steps on how to shift from doing to leading:

- *Grow from specialist to generalist.* You have likely built a career based on your expertise of a specific function. It's now time to focus beyond that function and increase your knowledge of the entire organization. You will need to learn how the function you lead impacts other areas of the business and how your team can better support those areas to achieve organizational results. Create opportunities to spend time with other leaders in the organization. Pay attention to what is going on in the business at every level, including the impact on the customer. Don't lose sight of the "portrait" view but invest heavily in gaining the "panoramic" view.

- *Develop the skill of delegating.* Delegating is not simply telling someone else to do something you cannot or don't want to do. Delegating requires identifying the person who can best accomplish a task and teaching them to do it, holding them accountable for doing it, and offering feedback and recognition when they have done it. Good delegation requires a level of trust and the leadership maturity to know that something doesn't have to be done exactly the way you would do it to be effective.

- *Maximize team capability.* When everyone on the team is assigned the appropriate task and the leader is casting vision, setting strategy, sharing in goal setting, and scoring the results, the team is operating at its optimal level. When an entire organization operates in this way, it creates competitive advantage. The benefits are healthier leaders and more engaged teams.

- *Make it all about the team.* When you become a leader, it is no longer about you. It is about the team and the individuals entrusted to you. From that moment on, "you" don't accomplish anything. Together, "we" can accomplish everything. When the team achieves its goals, give its member the credit. When the team fails, accept all the responsibility. Find satisfaction in the success of the team and its members. You are no longer evaluated on completing a to-do list but instead on your ability to grow your team and create more leaders.

Growing yourself as a leader requires the self-awareness to change and the willingness to act. Shifting from doing to leading is critical to strengthening your leadership effectiveness.

Joy was an incredible engineer. She was recruited to her job in the middle of her junior year of college, and she was not a disappointment to her company. Known for hitting her targets month after month and achieving the highest performance ratings, she was promoted to leadership of a team early in her career. Equipped with only a two-day "Leadership 101" orientation provided by her firm, Joy took over a small team in one of the highest-producing divisions.

Within weeks, Joy was floundering in her new role, and she knew it. She was working around the clock trying to compensate for the gap left on the team when she moved into leadership. The team was not producing as well as when she was in her previous role, and the team members were frustrated and becoming quickly disengaged. Fortunately for Joy, she had formed a relationship with a trusted advisor within the firm who helped her overcome her early missteps and get back on a solid leadership track.

Her advisor counseled her to start by identifying the various roles on the team and asking the team to help her decide who should fill each role. From there, the team set goals together and determined how they would measure and communicate results to each other and eventually to senior management. As they assigned the goals and roles, the only role for Joy was to lead. She was accountable for keeping the vision in front of the team, monitoring progress, and removing barriers and obstacles that might hinder the team. Additionally, she coached the team members who needed to develop capacity and competency in their roles; she did not take over the work or assign any tasks to herself.

During her career, Joy repeated this process with every new promotion, and it eventually led to her leading the largest division of the firm with over thirty-five hundred employees. She credits her success to those early days when she learned how to move from doing to leading.

Lead a Team

Entire libraries are dedicated to the topic of leadership. In fact, the best leaders continuously learn from other great leaders. The intention here is to prepare you for the day you are entrusted with a group of people to lead. Nothing prepares someone to lead as much as the actual experience of leading. As you focus on growing your career and if becoming a leader is a goal, then do everything you can to prepare yourself for your first experience. It is often the first experience that determines career success.

Imagine this: *You are sitting one day in a cubicle working on a project or perhaps working remotely at the local coffee shop. The work you are doing is compelling, exciting even. The boss is amazing, and your teammates inspire you with their creativity and innovation. You are building the career of which you always dreamed. Toying with the idea of eventually being a leader, you've attended a few seminars and read a handful of books. Then a calendar invite shows up in your inbox. Your boss has requested time with you the next day.*

Your mind quickly races through your assignments and projects to see if you are behind on anything. After affirming in your own mind that all is well, you confirm that you will be at the meeting. You know things are going well, so you anticipate an additional assignment or perhaps feedback about a current project. Receiving a promotion to lead a team doesn't cross your mind as you sip your skinny vanilla latte with no whip.

By the end of the next day, your world has changed. You have a new role and now have responsibility for eight team members. It's exciting to receive recognition and a promotion, but it feels a bit overwhelming too. There are many leadership-development programs that prepare emerging leaders for their futures. However, many do not, and as has been said, often the best performers are promoted with little or no training. So what do you do first?

Beginning a new role as a leader is much like the first ninety days on any new job. Understanding expectations and setting goals are the first steps. Hopefully, when the role is assigned to you, that is the initial discussion you have with your new boss. Beyond that, the next step is to assess the talent you have available to meet those expectations and achieve the goals.

Meeting one-on-one with every new team member should help you get to know them individually and learn about their goals and desires. Ask about their on-the-job successes, disappointments, career goals, preferred communication styles, and preferred form of recognition (public or private). If the team has participated in any personality assessments, such as the Enneagram, Myers-Briggs Type Indicator, DISC, or Predictive Index, ask them to share the results with you and be prepared to share your results in return.

The first team meeting is an important opportunity for you to communicate your vision, goals, and expectations for the team. Prepare carefully, ensuring that you have included the team's input in each of these areas. Also, observe the group environment. Are there behaviors you want to recognize so that they are repeated? Are there unhealthy behaviors you want to address immediately so that they do not continue and negatively impact the new team?

After assessing talent and setting team direction, assign roles to the new team. The information gathered in your interviews may provide insight on adjustments that need to be made within the team. Don't be afraid to make changes, but do so carefully and with input from key stakeholders.

Once the team members are settled in their new roles and the vision has been cast for the direction of the team, ensure that the team is working together effectively. Team-building days or retreats are great ways to kick off new working relationships and help everyone move in the same direction.

The next step is to intentionally create the elements of the team culture with the members. The team-building day or retreat is an ideal time to begin this exercise. Discuss the purpose of the team, understanding why the team exists. Create a challenging mission that describes what the team does and the major goal they are trying to achieve. Craft core values that the team believes are critical to how they will work together and serve others.

As you begin leading individual team members, help them create goals for themselves on which performance will be evaluated. Ensure complete clarity of role and goals from the very beginning. Be prepared to hold them accountable, and provide feedback when needed. Be clear about how they can access your assistance when needed. Should they drop in to see you, text, call, or email? Be accessible and available. You will earn respect if they can reach you when they need to.

Schedule regular one-on-one meetings with each team member. Create a format for the meeting that includes updates on work, feedback on projects, and questions about how you can help them. Empower them as much as possible to solve their own problems, and they will grow into employees you can trust and to whom you can delegate.

In most cases, a leader cannot communicate too much. Your team will want to hear from you, likely often. They desire the same communication you seek from your leader. They want to know how the organization is performing, what's important to leadership, what leadership knows about their work, what changes to anticipate, and even what's happening within the industry. A transparent leader is a trusted leader. Within reason, share as much as possible with your team to keep them engaged.

Leadership is not just about what you do but even more so about who you are. Be respectful, accountable, decisive, transparent, honest, and caring. This list of what to do and who to be is not all-inclusive, but it is a very good start to growing your new leadership career.

Lead through Change

In a previous chapter we discussed how to navigate change for ourselves. When we assume a leadership position, one of our most significant responsibilities is to lead followers through a season of change.

Change is essential to growth. The greater the growth, the greater the change required. Embracing change on an individual level is truthfully a lifelong practice, but if you are tasked with leading a team, the process often accelerates. Your goal is to find a graceful pace through changes and to avoid stagnation at all costs, as it will threaten even the best teams.

> Kristin led a large function within a rapidly growing organization. As a pioneer in the organization and an early leader of her function, she had built the structure, systems, and processes to support the body of work. However, after over twenty years of leadership, Kristin had transformed the function and had selected, grown, and developed a team that was ready for more responsibility. For Kristin's own growth, it was time for a change, and she began to think about options that would provide the opportunity for her and others to grow.
>
> For Kristin, the most difficult part of change was not deciding what she *would* do next but in helping her team discover what they *could* do in the next season with healthy change management.

Maybe you have been in a similar place and wonder how you can help lead and manage change with your team. Following are some suggestions:

- *Be clear.* Explaining change with clarity is paramount for successful change management. Be sure all the decisions related to the change have been made and that there is a consistent and clear message to communicate the change to everyone impacted directly or indirectly.

- *Counsel individuals one-on-one about change that impacts their work.* Consider not only the work impact but also the social impact of the change. Hearing about change for the first time in the presence of others is often difficult. Show respect by ensuring that no one is surprised about what impacts them most.

- *Make no assumptions about individual responses to change.* Everyone responds differently. Give each person time and space to process their thoughts, feelings, and ideas. The greater the change, the more time needed. Some need to process alone, and others need to talk through what they have heard. Give space and be available.

- *Cast a vision for the next season of opportunity.* Growth requires change, and change fuels growth. As long as that cycle continues, there is limitless opportunity for the business and staff. Be prepared to help others see the vision of where the change is taking the organization and what their opportunities are in the new season.

- *Constantly adjust development plans to prepare others for change and new opportunities.* Don't wait until a change is needed to prepare others for change. Continuously prepare for growth and change by honing and developing the skills of all the talent available to you.

- *Display the courage to move on at the right time.* While displaying patience for others to process change is vital to healthy change management, it is also important to make the call when it is time for everyone to move on. Allow for feelings of loss, grief, anxiety, challenge, and excitement to run their course. But when it's time to move on, it's time. Be courageous and lead the way for your team.

- *Make your decisions right.* One of my mentors often told me, "You won't always make the right decisions, so make your decisions right." When making change-related decisions, sometimes the leader gets it wrong. If you make a mistake, correct it. Don't get stuck in the wrong decision. Do what you need to do to make it right.

* *Prepare for the next change.* If your organization keeps growing, it must change at the rate of growth. The more you grow, the faster the pace of change. Prepare yourself and your team to meet the ever-changing demands of growth. You will stay ahead of the curve, and your organization will win.

Personal development author Dan Millman writes, "To rid yourself of old patterns, focus all of your energy not on fighting the old, but on building the new."[4] As leaders, it is our role to move our teams in the healthiest way possible from the old to the new. In that process, preserve the core of the culture and usher people carefully and intentionally into a new vision of the best future. Successful organizations develop and strengthen the muscle of this skill to grow their teams and create resiliency to sustain the organization for the future. Teams that are hopeful about what's next are more adaptable to change.

Lead with Hope

"Hope is not a strategy," I was once told. No, it certainly is not, but hope is vital to the effectiveness of a great leader. Without hope, how do we dare to envision a future better than the present? Without hope, how do we encourage our teams to manage adversity? Without hope, how do we invest our lives in something bigger than ourselves? Without hope, we are unable to inspire, develop, and launch other leaders.

Impactful leaders know the importance of finding hope, keeping hope, and sharing hope in order to inspire their teams to new levels of success and influence. Consider the following three ways to instill, preserve, and multiply hope among your team members:

* *Discover the hope for those you lead.* If we have no hope for the people who serve with us, how can we expect them to have

hope for the potential impact of the organization? Find the greatness within each team member and develop it, leverage it, and maximize their chances to display it. The opportunities are limitless for those who know that someone believes in them. Our team members don't need a fan club, but they do need at least one person who will acknowledge their capabilities and the possibility of success within their reach.

- *Demonstrate your hope in others, and help them find hope for themselves.* Cultivate an abundance mentality within your team so that each member believes in the opportunity to grow, achieve, and win, both individually and as a team. Leaders with abundance mentality ensure that their team knows there is plenty of opportunity for everyone and that they do not foster unnecessary and distracting competition. For vision to be sustainable, every team member needs to possess hope for themselves and their own future. When everyone finds their own hope and is vested in a shared vision or goal, the team and organization are far more successful.

- *Advocate for the hope you see in your team or staff.* Be the champion, sponsor, or mentor that a young leader needs to progress on the path. Call out the competency and capability you see and nurture it. Help others to see and embrace it as well. It is a disservice to those we lead if we are the only ones to see hope in their future. We set up a more successful future for the people entrusted to us when others have hope in them too. This is especially true for people who will be part of a future we are not likely to see.

In a previous chapter, I shared the story of Justin Miller, who cofounded and now leads CARE for AIDS. The ministry has produced amazing results and changed tens of thousands of lives. Justin has inspired a generation to care for those who have little hope. He has inspired the leaders who work for him to lead with hope. When he first began the journey, hope for funds, hope for partnerships, hope for healing, and hope for the transformation of people's lives were all he had. He inspired others with that hope, and it took hold.

Leaders who want to create a better future do so by unharnessing hope and allowing it to take root, sprout, and flourish in their lives and the lives of their followers.

Solve Problems

One of my early mentors gave me some very wise counsel: the world will always need problem solvers. If you want to grow a career, becoming an effective problem solver is a good start. Work is full of opportunities to prevent and solve problems. Those who are exceptionally good at solving problems have a distinct advantage on the path to success. They often become leaders among their peers. The bigger the problems they can solve, the more they achieve and the more respect they earn.[5]

Most day-to-day decisions, except for those in the fields of medicine or emergency response, will not be life or death. Still, the ability to solve simple and complex problems is critical. Perhaps one of the most memorable on-the-job problem-solving examples comes from NASA's Apollo 13 failed space mission in 1970.

Due to an explosion in the command capsule, NASA had to abort the lunar landing and bring the astronauts home in the lunar module. The problem was that the lunar module was designed to hold two astronauts for thirty-six hours, not three astronauts for ninety-six hours. These conditions caused a life-threatening rise in carbon dioxide gas in the lunar capsule. With every breath, the astronauts were releasing poison back into the capsule.

The command module had filters to clean the air, but they were square. The lunar module used round filters. The square filters used in the command module would not fit into the round holes of the lunar module. As the astronauts faced the real possibility of death due to the dangerous levels of CO_2 in the lunar module, NASA's ground support was working around the clock to offer a solution.

The support team made a prototype out of materials the astronauts had onboard, using cardboard, duct tape, and socks to craft a makeshift filter. Then they had to instruct the astronauts how to construct the filter, even as they were battling the effects of carbon dioxide poisoning.[6]

While successful in making the filter and averting the crisis, they had several more problems to solve before they finally landed safely back to earth. Interestingly, part of the training for astronauts is to anticipate what could go wrong and create solutions to either save their lives or successfully complete the mission.

Problem solving is a skill that is certainly aided by intelligence but is not reliant on it. We can grow in this ability, and as we do, we will also grow our value to the organization. The following ten steps can help you solve the problems you face:

1. *Identify and define the problem.* A friend of mine often says, "A problem well defined is half solved." You cannot find the appropriate solution to the problem if you don't recognize and fully understand what the problem is.

2. *Redefine the problem as an opportunity.* Yes, some problems are problems, but many are opportunities for something better. Changing your mindset can help you think more clearly about solutions.

3. *Determine the root causes of the problem.* Start with why. Why is it a problem? Why did it occur? Without determining the root causes, you might resolve the symptoms but the problem would reoccur.

4. *Start with the end in mind.* It is possible to start with the idea of what needs to happen and reverse engineer to a solution. Understanding where you are headed will help you develop more viable solutions to the problem.

5. *Brainstorm solutions with others.* Brainstorming sessions should be wide open for idea generation. No idea is a bad

one while brainstorming. Capture every idea. There will be an opportunity for eliminating less-than-optimal solutions later in the process. Be sure to include people with diverse points of view in your brainstorming session.

6. *Experiment or pilot the most viable solutions.* We learned this in high school chemistry: as long as we didn't do something dangerous, we needed to experiment. Ask others for feedback for your proposed solutions. Run a market test. Consider various ideas and pilot them in real-life environments.

7. *Carefully evaluate the experiments, tests, and pilots.* Use data and qualitative feedback to determine your best course of action.

8. *Focus on the broader organizational strategy.* Don't become so wrapped up in your solution that you fail to consider the overall impact to the organization. The best solutions are not the ones that eliminate the difficulties for a few but elevate the possibilities for many.

9. *Work hard.* Problem solving is difficult. That is why problem solvers are in demand. Drive hard to solutions, and be ready to repeat the process often. Colonel Harlan Sanders did not found KFC until he was sixty-five years old. He tried more than a thousand recipes before a restaurant finally accepted one. Problem solvers are resilient.

10. *Measure results.* To become an effective problem solver means creating metrics that demonstrate your effectiveness. Did the solution work? Was the solution within budget? Did you meet your original goals and objectives? Don't forget to communicate the results to the stakeholders.

These ten steps provide a framework for solving the daily problems, opportunities, and challenges in your role. Become known as a great problem solver, and you will grow your career.

Tell Stories

Storytelling is one of the most effective ways leaders influence their teams. Especially effective is when leaders share personal and authentic stories of their own leadership. Stories provide a lesson that instructs people in how to make decisions on their own. If you want to grow a team that functions by commitment to principles rather than compliance to a stack of rules, it is important to be good at telling stories.

Good storytellers do not just convey information; they engage the energy and emotions of the listener. A story can stir the listener to the core and compel the listener to act. Stories can motivate a team member to accomplish a goal or convince a customer to buy a product or service. Connecting an idea with an emotion is more impactful than only communicating the specifications, requirements, and benefits.

Most importantly, as business communications expert, author, and storyteller Carmine Gallo states, "Storytelling is not something we do. Storytelling is something we are."[7] When you are attempting to motivate a team member or an entire team, sharing your experiences and the experiences of others you have observed is a powerful tool. If you do it often enough, you are no longer someone who tells stories but someone who is a storyteller.

Stories are generated from personal experiences—what we read and view and what others tell us. If you are a new leader, sharing with your team about your own experiences, especially your learning opportunities, stories about the earlier years of the organization, and the successes of others, helps them better understand you as a leader. The more they understand you, the more likely they are to trust you. Gaining trust is essential to growing a career.

> Long before he was likely ready, Adam took over a large department in his organization. Circumstances in his company accelerated his career trajectory, and suddenly,

without adequate preparation, he was thrust into leadership of two hundred employees. He held information close to the vest and was not very approachable.

His interactions with the team were often awkward, and he struggled in individual conversations. Then one day he put an unusual piece of furniture in his office. It was an old and scarred office chair. It looked to be a lot less comfortable than the ergonomically correct chair that was previously in his office. His team was curious.

He explained that the chair belonged to the first president of the company. From that chair, he began to tell stories of the company culture, its history, and the people who had made them so successful. Soon an old conference table showed up in his office. It was definitely something out of the 1950s. He explained that the leadership of the company gathered around that table to discuss the fate of the organization when they thought they might lose the business. It was at that time and at that table that they created the core values of the organization. These values united the employees and enabled them to create a new focus that kept them in business for decades.

After experiencing success telling other people's stories, Adam eventually began to tell more stories about himself and what his early career taught him. In doing so, he made himself vulnerable to his team, and the trust between his team and him began to grow. Soon, he adopted the storytelling skill of making his team and their customers the hero of his stories. It transformed his leadership. People trusted him, and they became loyal followers.

If you want to grow your career, develop the skill of storytelling. Pursue it for the purpose of not just occasionally telling a good story but to teach, develop, and grow others by motivating them with the lessons your stories tell.

Become a Mentor

The most important role of a leader is developing more leaders. Organizations rely on the availability of leaders to grow and succeed. Nothing will grow your own career more than being known for creating other leaders. You can begin developing other leaders before you ever hold a leadership position by becoming a mentor to others.

Mentors form one-on-one relationships and help others learn, transfer knowledge, remove obstacles and barriers, and open doors of opportunities. Mentoring someone can be a valuable experience, but it requires focus and intentionality. A great mentor guides the mentee through difficult situations and learning opportunities and helps the mentee achieve goals and reach full potential.

Samantha was tapped to be a mentor within her organization. This was particularly exciting news because she was not a supervisor yet, and she realized that the organization was providing a skill-building opportunity for her. While her first priority was to help make her mentee successful, her second priority was to specifically grow leadership skills to prepare her for a future leadership role.

After interviewing a few mentors and mentees, she assessed what skills she needed to focus on to provide the best experience for her mentee. She then took the additional steps to receive feedback from her supervisor, her own mentor, and several of her peers to determine the skills she needed to develop during the assignment. With her plan in place, she was enthusiastic about getting started with her new mentee, Jessie.

The first skill for Samantha to improve was *listening*. Good mentors are good listeners. They actively listen by looking others straight in the eye and providing nonverbal cues, such as nodding, smiling, and leaning in while the mentee is talking. An effective mentor will avoid distractions and interruptions while meeting with a mentee. A good listener puts the phone on silent and doesn't glance at incoming texts on her smart watch. Mentoring Jessie gave Samantha an opportunity to practice being a better listener, which would serve her well throughout her career.

For Samantha to be a strong future leader, she needed to improve her abilities to *cast a vision*, *create a strategy*, and *inspire others to follow*. Working with Jessie would give her an opportunity to grow these skills as she helped Jessie cast a vision for her future and create a strategy to achieve it. They began with the end in mind by clearly creating a goal for their work together. Then they decided the tactics to help them achieve the goal. Jessie's goal was to be promotable at the end of their assignment together. They discussed the tactics needed for Jessie to reach her goal: what she needed to learn and how she could apply what she learned.

Providing feedback was a skill with which Samantha had very little experience, but feedback was something Jessie would need to achieve her goal. Serving as a mentor gave Samantha the opportunity to learn how to have crucial conversations and give candid and helpful feedback. For the benefit of both, the women agreed that providing feedback would be a high priority for the time they spent together.

Already known for her strong *decision-making skills*, Samantha had to remember that her job was to listen and coach Jessie, not make decisions for her. People don't grow without the opportunity to make their own decisions and reap the rewards for the good ones and experience the consequences for the poor ones. A good mentor never tells a mentee what to do but instead encourages curiosity about the options and serves as a sounding board as the mentee considers the choices.

Networking was the final skill on which Samantha decided to focus. She had been fortunate in her career to have mentors who helped her meet people and to have experiences that helped her grow. It was time for her to do that for someone else. Inviting Jessie to meetings with other leaders, traveling to meet key clients, and recommending her for special projects were just a few of the ways Samantha planned to encourage and help Jessie.

Samantha and Jessie met twice each month for a year, once in person for two hours and a one-hour phone call. Additionally, they met once per month for lunch with different leaders in the organization, and by planning well in advance, Jessie was able to accompany Samantha on two business trips. By the end of the assignment twelve months later, Jessie was far more entrenched in company culture, had gained credibility in her work, and had developed new skills. Samantha had not only helped Jessie become promotable, but she too became promotable as she gained valuable leadership competencies through the assignment. As it turned out, Jessie was promoted to a new role and her new leader had also been recently promoted—Samantha!

This is in no way an exhaustive list of behaviors that help people become strong leaders, but they are a few of the skills that are important to begin developing early in order to grow your career.

The most meaningful sermon I ever heard was delivered decades ago by A. L. Patterson.[8] The premise of the entire sermon was about a man mentioned only twice in the Bible. His name is Shamgar, and Judges 3:31 records that he killed six hundred Philistines with an ox goad and saved Israel. In his sermon, Patterson pointed out how Shamgar defeated the Philistines: he started where he was—a man with a God-appointed mission. He used what he had—an ox goad. He did what he could—obeyed and charged into battle. It was enough for him to accomplish his role.

Using the words of A. L. Patterson, I encourage you to do the same as you grow your career. *Start where you are.* Use whatever opportunity you are given and make the most of it. *Use what you have.* Apply the abilities you were born with, the skills you have acquired, and the tools you have picked up along the way. Finally, *do what you can.* Lean into the opportunity and give it all of your effort. I believe it will be enough to help you find and keep a job you love and grow a fulfilling career.

WHAT'S MY STORY?

1. What am I doing today to prepare me to lead others in the future? What skills am I developing?
2. Do I inspire others? Is there any area lacking in my integrity that I need to improve before being selected to lead others?
3. What tasks do I need to delegate so that I can focus more on leading and less on "doing"?
4. Am I open to change and capable of leading others through change? What biases toward change do I need to eliminate to be a better change agent?
5. Do I communicate a hopeful future among my team members? How can I better lead with hope?
6. Have I developed a framework for solving problems? What is my personal process for problem solving?
7. What personal stories should I consider telling so that others can learn from me in the future?
8. Who needs me to mentor them? What skills do I need to focus on and grow to be an effective mentor?

LEAVE A JOB

PART IV

Most people work to make a living, but for some, the work is a calling that drives them to both do more and be more. A job is only something that is listed on a résumé, but a calling, once we find it, is something we pursue heartily because it resonates in our soul.

Finding a job within your calling is the sweet spot and is much more difficult to part ways with. If your job is only a job, perhaps you don't love it anymore, and you might even be making yourself miserable. If you are on the verge of breaking up with your job, following are some questions you may want to consider:

- *Do you have a meaningful purpose in your job?* A purpose calls you to something bigger than yourself and can provide lasting value beyond the work you do every day.
- *Do you have a mission in your job?* What is your goal, and where are you headed? Does your job help direct you to your ultimate career goals? Does it help you become a better person on your path to achieving your career goals?

- *Do you enjoy the people you work with daily?* Do they enrich your life and help you become a better person and a better member of the team? Perhaps the job you have in this season serves you best simply because of the people you are meeting. If your job allows you to be surrounded by great leaders and coworkers who are making an imprint on your life and helping you grow, you might be in the right place for now.

- *Does the work resonate with your core values?* Do you continue to be proud of the work you do and the organization for which you work? Do the people you work with help you live out your own core values? The founder of a company I worked for told me often, "Be careful with whom you associate yourself because you will become like that person." I left my first career job because it was a mismatch with my core values. I stayed for thirty-three years in another career position because it was a solid fit with my core values.

- *Can you reinvent the work you do to better fit your interests and your goals?* What can you learn today to enhance your job to make it more interesting and boost your own performance? For years, I did similar work. With scope and scale and new learning, it changed over time, but the basic function and expertise required remained the same. So I pursued a different role within the organization. I had to reinvent myself, but the new challenges led me to new goals and the opportunity to explore new subjects and fresh dreams.

If you can answer these questions affirmatively, then you might be poised to fall in love with your work all over again.

Like any other passion in our lives, work has to be nurtured and cultivated, or we will be in danger of losing our love for it. Few people would ever claim that work is the most important priority in life. However, it is the way we provide for ourselves and our families and contribute to the marketplace and our communities.

With the amount of time that we spend working, it's a worthwhile mission to fall in love with our jobs—except when we don't. And then it is time to move on to the next opportunity.

10

Changing Jobs

For one reason or another, the time may come to seek a new job. It may be due to normal life transitions, such as graduating from college, obtaining an advanced degree, or the relocation of a spouse. It may be that the company is going out of business or the job itself is not a good fit or the organization did not turn out to be the kind of employer that was expected. People may decide to leave if they see no opportunity for advancement, receive poor training, or feel devalued and unrecognized. Sometimes they leave because of a poor leader or due to an opportunity for advancement elsewhere. Still others leave to start their own organization.

> Late one afternoon, I received a phone call from my young friend Brett. A member of Gen Z, Brett is newer to the workforce and had been at his present company for only twelve months. Interning the summer before graduation gave Brett an inside look at the company he had decided to join, but a recent buyout of his tech firm left him disillusioned. While some of the younger technical staff were

> retained by the new owner, much of the leadership had been replaced.
>
> The new ownership created a new culture, and it was not the familiar one Brett was attracted to during his internship. Also, he heard rumors that his division might be reorganized and that his job might eventually be eliminated. Having never been in such a situation, Brett wondered aloud what he should do.

It is always ideal to find a new job before leaving a current one. But it is also more difficult to pursue a new job while currently employed. When you decide to pursue a new job, there are several steps you can take to prepare yourself. Planning well will make your job search and the transition much smoother.

If you anticipate a job change, save some of your personal leave time to use for interviewing. Making excuses to your current boss about being late to work or even telling an untruth about missing work creates a lot of anxiety and does not position you to be at your best in an interview. The stress can be avoided by planning ahead and reserving some leave time.

Of course, revising your résumé by updating your experience and acquired skills is important. Keep your online profiles updated as well so that recruiters will have your most current qualifications and can easily contact you. Your social media is a reflection of your personal brand, so be sure it positively reflects your character and competency. If you are ready to actively search for a job, you may want to reach out to recruiters.

Connect with your contacts, including your college alumni networks and your professional group associations, and begin to network for job opportunities. If you do not want your current employer to know about your job search, be discrete and carefully consider whom you will inform of your intentions.

As you prepare to search for a new job, consider key issues ahead of time. Are you willing to relocate? If so, where? When asked, who can you provide as a reference? What benefits are not negotiable in a new job?

These are all actions Brett took as he prepared to search for a new job. Once his résumé and profiles were updated, he participated in some mock interviews with me. It had been awhile since he had interviewed for a job, and refreshing his skills gave him more confidence that he was ready to reenter the job market.

Resign and Give Notice

How we leave a job is as important as how we start one. At some point in the future, you are likely to need a reference from a current employer. If you find a new job within the same industry, you may work with some of the same people or they may be a client one day. Whatever the case, you want to leave a positive impression. The following tips will help you leave a job with your reputation and credibility intact:

- *Resign in person.* This may seem obvious, but in this digital world, people sometimes consider it acceptable to email, text, or phone in a resignation. If you want to remain well thought of, and you do, then schedule a time to talk to your boss face-to-face. For virtual roles, you may have to resign on a video call.

- *Submit a written letter of resignation following the face-to-face meeting.* Even if you and your boss have a great relationship, it is beneficial to you to have a written record that you chose to leave of your own accord.

- *Provide ample notice, which is customarily a minimum of two weeks.* Your boss may choose to send you on your way immediately, but the respectful action is to give notice. If the boss wants you to work out your notice, give 100 percent until your exit is complete. If the company wants you to stay longer, it's best not to extend it past four weeks. They need to move on with selecting and training someone else for the role, and you need to move on to your new job. Enthusiasm on everyone's part—you, your current employer, and your future employer—will begin to decrease if you stay too long.

- *Don't burn any bridges.* This old cliché is a good one to remember. Even if asked during an exit interview, don't bash the company or any of its employees. Offer positive statements about the parts of your experience that you enjoyed and constructive feedback on what might have made the job better. Do so while maintaining the highest level of professionalism.
- *Offer to train your successor.* If the company selects someone to replace you before you leave, offer to help train the new employee. Again, the boss might decline the offer, but you will be more highly thought of by offering to help the organization continue to be successful.
- *Ask your employer for a letter of recommendation or permission to list them as a reference in the future.*
- *Thank your boss and your organization* for the opportunity to work for the company. Even if you had a poor experience, hopefully you obtained some training and skills on which to build for the future. Be grateful and gracious.
- *Return all company property promptly.* It hurts your reputation if the company must hunt you down to retrieve a security badge, parking pass, computer, key, or other company-issued equipment. Protect your own integrity by voluntarily returning these items when you leave. Only take personal items that are rightfully yours.

Leaving well, without baggage, sets you up for success in the next opportunity. You can start your new job ready to go and ready to grow in the next chapter of your career.

Prevent a Termination

In today's marketplace where there is less employee-employer mutual loyalty, the brutal truth is that many of us will get fired at some point in our careers. Getting fired is actually quite common. Many business icons have been famously fired during their careers.

Bernie Marcus and Arthur Blank were corporate officers of Handy Dan, a home improvement chain. A corporate raider fired both of them, which took them by surprise as they had helped to make Handy Dan very successful. They used their retail knowledge and partnered together to start their own discount home improvement store chain, the Home Depot. In their first decade in business, they opened over one hundred stores and made more than $2.7 billion in sales. The company that fired them, Handy Dan, closed in 1989.[1]

Walt Disney was fired by the *Kansas City Star* because he lacked creativity and "had no good ideas." He went on to open an animation studio, but it failed because he lacked business skills. He partnered with his brother, Roy Disney, a business leader, and they began Disney Brothers Studios. It was there that he created Mickey Mouse, started Disney World, and won twenty-two Academy Awards.[2]

Oprah Winfrey was believed to be too emotional and was fired by Baltimore's WJZ-TV as a news anchor. Rather than buying out her $25,000 contract, they placed Winfrey on an afternoon talk show. *Business Week* called her the "greatest Black philanthropist in American history," and Forbes listed her as the "richest African-American of the 20th century."[3]

While sometimes we have no control over the circumstances leading to a termination, such as a layoff, there are certainly behaviors that are more likely to contribute to being fired. The most obvious of these are illegal activities and character failure. Stealing from the organization, lying to the boss or clients, bullying, and sexual harassment all fall into these two categories.

One of the most common reasons people are fired is because of a personality clash. Perhaps the boss and employee or the employee and team made a poor assessment of chemistry fit during selection, or personalities evolved over time and no longer fit well together. In some cases, a new boss comes in to take over and the chemistry is not there.

A lack of competency is the third reason people are often fired from a job. This can be a result of poor selection, but more often it is because the employee is not applying the competencies they possess. Failing to show up for meetings or arrive to work on time is a way of displaying poor time management. Inadequate or weak communication skills and resisting accountability can also lead to termination. Often, it is a combination of these factors over time.

In summary, consider these dos and don'ts to avoid being fired:

- Never lie, cheat, or steal at work (or anywhere).
- Don't be a bully.
- Keep your hands to yourself.
- Watch your words, and don't use inappropriate language or make jokes that are in bad taste.
- Don't avoid your boss; engage often.
- Show up every day, and show up on time or early.
- When you are unable to be at work, communicate to your boss and team.
- Communicate the status of your work to your boss and team.
- Be accountable, and do what you are asked to do and then some.
- Own your mistakes and don't make excuses when you fail.

Following these ten suggestions is not a guarantee that you will never be fired, but failure to follow them certainly increases the likelihood of being fired.

Survive a Termination

Like most events in life, what happens to us is not nearly as important as how we respond to what happens to us. Sometimes, despite our best efforts, we find ourselves in difficult situations. One of life's biggest disappointments is losing a job. If this happens to you, don't let discouragement overwhelm you. It's time to find another job. While it may be painful at the time, it is just another step on your path in navigating what's next.

When you are informed of your termination, the first thing you want to do is ask good questions to understand the why behind the decision. Hopefully, the firing does not come as a complete surprise, but if it does, don't freeze and don't panic. Try to learn something from the experience that can help you as you move forward. Learn where you failed to meet the organization's expectations and what they believe you could have done differently.

Ask your employer if they will provide you a letter of reference. If your reason for termination is a layoff due to restructuring or a poor job fit, it is more likely they will do so. Also ask particular peers and supervisors if they would be willing to provide a reference for you in the future. If a severance is being offered, try to negotiate what will be said about your performance in the severance agreement. Ask your employer to provide outplacement services as part of your severance. Generally, they can be expensive, but the help will be invaluable in making a career transition in the face of a termination. If you have health benefits, negotiate to continue those for a period of time.

Severance pay is typically one to two weeks for every year worked, but it can be more. The general practice is to try to negotiate four weeks of severance pay for each year worked. Middle managers and executives usually receive a higher amount.[4] Often, if an employee is terminated for a reason other than job performance, such as theft or excessive absenteeism, severance pay is not offered.

Once you have left your job, be still for a little while and take a break. Give the news a few days to settle in, then start planning your move forward. You want to be clearheaded as you approach the job market. This is a great opportunity to think about what you want in your next job. What did you love about your previous one, and what did you dislike? If you feel stuck, ask for help. Many companies specialize in career transition and can help you find your way to your next role. Job and career websites, such as Monster.com, Indeed, Glassdoor, and LinkedIn, can help you locate these resources. Update your online profiles to let people know you are available. Reach out to the networks you have built during your career to see who is looking for talent. Post-termination is a good time to attend industry conferences and local chapter meetings of your membership networks to help you make connections for your job search.

It is easy to feel isolated after unexpectedly losing a job. Try to remain active during your job search. You might consider volunteer work as a way of staying connected with people. Spending time with family and friends and staying physically active will help to alleviate some of the discouragement and stress that are likely after being terminated from a job. Discouragement will prevent you from performing at your best and projecting a positive outlook when you interview for a new job.

Consider taking temporary or contract positions to stay active in the job market while you search for a permanent position. Do everything you can to exceed expectations in your temporary role to create a positive reference to use in your job search.

The most important thing to remember is that you will get through it and, hopefully, find a new job that is fulfilling and supports your career growth. In his book *You'll Get through This*, Max Lucado writes, "You'll get through this. It won't be painless. It won't be quick. But God will use this mess for good. In the meantime, don't be foolish or naïve. But don't despair either. With God's help, you'll get through this."[5] There are many things we have to "get through" this side of heaven, and losing a job is a difficult one. However, it is just a setback. You can overcome it, find and keep a new job, and grow a career.

Retire

When you decided to read this book, you likely did not choose it because you were thinking of retiring. In fact, you probably chose this book because you are trying to find a job, keep a job, and grow a career. To you, retirement is decades away and not on your radar for navigating what is next. However, if you ever wish to retire, today is the best time to start thinking about it.

Some people plan never to retire, but it's always good to have options. There are still a few professions in which retirement is mandatory. Your health or the health of a family member might also require you to retire at a younger age than expected. As much as you might enjoy your career now, an irresistible opportunity may come along later that changes your mind. That is exactly what happened to me.

At an age much younger than when most people contemplate retiring, I was presented with an incredible opportunity. My company presented its first ever Voluntary Early Retirement Option (VERO) to a large number of tenured employees. Unlike some programs in some organizations, this one was truly voluntary. I could have continued to enjoy my career in the company I loved, but I was presented with an opportunity that would both provide for my needs and allow me to follow some of the other dreams in my life.

Retiring early was one of the most difficult decisions I have made in life. Our company had a mandatory retirement age of sixty-five for officers, so for years I had a date in mind as to when I would leave the organization. The retirement option was far in advance of that date. After thirty-three years of literally growing up in an organization and creating thousands of relationships in the process, it was hard to imagine leaving it behind and doing something else.

One of the first actions I took to help me make the decision was to reach out to a trusted advisor. She helped me assess my current state in some specific areas to determine if I was ready to retire from my first career. There are likely many more considerations for most people, but we focused on three.

Financial

While money is not the most important consideration for most decisions, when it comes to retirement, there really are not many options if we are not financially prepared. I recommend several behaviors early in your career that will prepare you to take advantage of unexpected opportunities later in life.

- *Live below your means and stay out of debt.* When you finally land your first career job and begin making a regular paycheck, it's easy to fall into the trap of buying now and paying later. After all, you expect that another check will come about every two weeks, so why not go ahead and spend the money now? The problem with that mindset is that you continue to repeat the pattern until the debt exceeds your ability to repay it. In the meantime, you pay more in interest rates. Taking a personal financial-management course, such as Dave Ramsey's Financial Peace University, early in your career can help you set and achieve realistic financial goals.
- *Save, save, save and then save some more.* A rule of thumb is to save at least ten percent of your income. On top of that, I recommend that you invest the maximum amount allowed by law into a retirement account. This is even more advantageous if your company has a matching retirement plan. Save cash for emergencies and to make debt-free purchases. Save as much as you can to fund your post-career life.
- *Give some away.* Giving to others will enrich your life and leave a lasting legacy. Often, giving blesses the giver as much as the receiver. The first year my husband and I were married, we committed to giving at least 10 percent of what was

then a very meager income. Still, we were committed to the principle of giving. When tax filing season rolled around after that first year, we witnessed what we considered a miracle. Our outgo exceeded our income. However, somehow, we had paid every bill and fulfilled our giving commitment. We don't give expecting anything in return, but we have certainly seen our giving multiplied and returned to us in unexpected ways.

- *Find a trusted financial advisor.* A financial advisor can assist you in planning the life you want by helping you determine how to meet your long-term goals of buying a home, educating children, starting your own business, and preparing for the lifestyle you desire in retirement. These are just a few of the services provided by a financial advisor. Find one who aligns with your values, and take advantage of their expertise to create a financial plan for your life.

When my husband and I married, we had one used car and a furnished one-room apartment. Since the car was financed, we really only owned the furniture, and it was a wedding gift. The only financial coaching we received was by observing our parents, who did four things: worked hard, paid their bills, saved money, and gave generously. We tried to do the same.

There is no real shortcut to building a healthy financial future. You might receive a financial windfall that seems to meet your every need, but even then, if you don't manage it well, it will be gone quickly. Most people who have the financial resources for retirement do so because they started early, made a plan, and managed it well.

Emotional

Surprisingly, the beginning of a career is also a good time to prepare emotionally for retirement. Over the course of their careers, many people identify themselves by vocation. Whether sitting next to someone on a plane, attending a dinner party, or networking at a conference, inevitably someone will ask the question "What do you do?"

Allowing our identities to be consumed by our professions sets us up for a crisis when the identity is no longer our vocation for whatever reason. However, this is especially true at retirement. Consider two scenarios.

Due to company requirements, a high-level executive had to retire before he was prepared emotionally. Over the course of his entire career, his identity had been connected to his senior-leadership position and all the benefits and perks associated with the job. When he retired, he was unable to separate himself from that identity and create a new one. He had a big family and the financial means to do most anything he wanted, but he found no joy in either of these because he could not let go of the desire to be viewed in his executive role.

Another man found himself in the same situation. However, over the course of his lengthy career, he prepared for that time when he would transition to a new season. He balanced his life between his relationships and his responsibilities. When he retired, he was able to more easily transition to the next chapter. He left his old life behind, traveled the country with his wife, and spent time with his children and grandchildren.

Social

Unless we already work remotely, one of the biggest adjustments in retirement is to the absence of the presence of people. Whether we physically go into an office or take part in conference calls and video chats with coworkers and clients, we are accustomed to connecting with someone almost every day. In retirement, the loss of that engagement can feel very isolating. Developing hobbies and interests over our lifetimes that involve interactions with others is good preparation for retirement. In this season, socialization requires far more intentionality than when working day after day in the marketplace.

Financial, emotional, and social issues are all considerations when deciding to retire. Whether due to resignation, termination, or retirement, the process of finding a new way to invest our lives that matches our purpose begins again. Leaving a job gives us the chance to apply what we have learned in the previous job to our next role.

Jenny worked for a company she loved, but she had outgrown her role, and her boss seemed reluctant to help her advance in the organization. She had done a great job and had earned his confidence, and he did not want to lose her. As much as she loved the company, she knew she had to grow, even if it meant leaving it.

One last time, Jenny approached her boss, Raphael, asking for his support in posting for an internal move. He dragged his feet and never seemed to get around to writing a recommendation for her. As a last-ditch effort, she visited the company's human resources department and asked one of the leaders if she could post for the job anyway. After learning that was not possible, she started contacting the recruiters who had been calling, emailing, and texting her. She updated her online career profiles and began her search.

Starting the process all over again, Jenny prepared for interviews by reviewing her résumé and identifying the skills, abilities, and interests she could bring to a new role and a new organization. She began lining up trusted individuals to act as references in her new job search. Wanting to protect her current job, she was able to find clients and former coworkers who could speak to her performance.

Soon, the interview requests flooded in, and Jenny was ready to find the next right job for her. Within weeks, she landed a new role that matched her interests, skills, and experiences perfectly. It was a promotion from her current role and seemed like the right move to advance her career.

Raphael was surprised when Jenny resigned and was grateful for the two-week notice she offered. He asked her to work out her notice to train others on the team to fulfill her role until a replacement could be selected. Because she had been a great performer and had demonstrated integrity in her leaving the organization, Raphael provided a letter of recommendation should she need it in the future. Jenny had successfully navigated leaving a job and finding a new job. She was now well on her way to growing her career.

Not all stories end so perfectly. There are bumps, twists, and turns on the path. Sometimes, a termination leads to a season of unemployment. Other times, just because a person desires to leave a job doesn't mean the perfect role is right around the corner. However, this book provides a road map to navigate your way to finding a job, keeping a job, and growing a career.

WHAT'S MY STORY?

1. Am I ready to consider a new job? Why do I want to change jobs? What will a new role or company provide me?
2. What do I need to update in preparation of searching for a new job?
3. Who do I need to contact and inform that I am in the job market?
4. What should I consider before I resign my current job? Benefits? Commute? Relocation?
5. What work habits do I need to change to prevent a termination? Is there anything in my character that I need to develop to prevent a termination?
6. What type of retirement do I desire? What will my life look like at retirement age? What kinds of things do I anticipate doing in retirement? How can I financially, emotionally, and socially prepare now for the season of retirement?

It Is All Going to Be OK

Late one evening, after an hour-long conversation with my youngest son, I hung up the phone and pondered deeply his answer to my last question. These late-night conversations occurred frequently. On the one hand, I was thankful that he felt the freedom to vent to me; on the other hand, I was concerned about his anxiety about the future—a trademark emotion of his generation. He has always been a driven, persistent, and resilient young man and, for the most part, successful at whatever he attempts. As a sophomore at a top university, he was facing adversity from every angle, causing him to doubt himself.

Six hours away, I sometimes feel helpless to offer him guidance. The irony that I was in the midst of writing this book while Trey, who has lived with me for twenty-one years and felt my influence every day, was struggling was not lost on me. Like every involved and caring parent, I want to fix it for him. I want him to see the amazing potential that I see in him and his brothers. Trey thinks my vision for him is clouded by parental bias. It's really not. I have evaluated tens of thousands of candidates over more than three decades. I know talent when I see it.

After many of these late-night conversations, in which Trey shared his worries about how he could possibly achieve his dreams in his circumstances, I finally asked him the question I should have asked him long before that night. I kept trying to solve his problems, give him answers, and almost command that he see the "ceiling and visibility unlimited" that I see for him. Finally, exhausted and out of suggestions, I asked an important question: "What can I do to help?" His answer was simple: "Tell me everything is going to be OK." He did not need me to tell him how it was going to be OK or what would happen next, he only needed my assurance that it will all work out in the end.

If you are like Trey and need to hear those words, please know that it is all going to be OK. Even in days of constant change, when it seems our world is falling apart, it will be OK. I cannot promise you that there will not be turbulence, cloudy skies, fog, and haze along the way. The human condition guarantees that we will experience discomfort, challenges, and trials. But I can tell you this about your career: when you put all the tools in this book to work for you, you will be doing the best you can. The "best you can do" is always enough. If you believe as I do that there is a chosen path for each of us, then using these tools and giving your best will keep you on that path.

If you find yourself straying from the path, come back to your purpose, mission, and core values and start again. Another path, meant just for you, will rise up to meet you. When things don't work out as I expect, I reflect on the possibility that I am being protected from something that will harm me or that something better will be provided to me. Ask yourself, Is this season of disappointment preparation for my next divine appointment?

The tools in this book are not designed to make you wealthy, assure that you'll be CEO of an organization, or place you on Fortune's 40 Under 40 list, although some or all of these accomplishments could certainly be realized. However, I am convinced that if you use these tools, you will find a calling that is fulfilling, work with organizations that help you reach your personal and professional dreams, and influence many people along the way. It's not an easy formula. Most of the best things in life are not easy, but they are usually worth it.

Now that you have finished this book, I hope you have confidence in your own talent and are ready to share it with the world. You might not be able to see it at this moment from where you sit, but I have been there with thousands of people and I can see it—ceiling and visibility unlimited. It's your CAVU. Go get it. I believe you can!

Recommended Resources

Books

Cheryl Bachelder, *Dare to Serve* (San Francisco: Berrett-Koehloer Publishers, 2018).

Jenny Blake, *Pivot: The Only Move That Matters Is Your Next One* (New York: Portfolio, 2016).

Brené Brown, *Daring Greatly* (New York: Avery, 2012).

Dale Carnegie, *How to Win Friends and Influence People* (New York: Simon & Schuster, rev. 2009).

Clayton Christensen, *How Will You Measure Your Life?* (New York: Harper Business, 2012).

James Clear, *Atomic Habits* (New York: Avery, 2016).

Henry Cloud, *Integrity: The Courage to Meet the Demands of Reality* (New York: HarperCollins, 2006).

Jim Collins, *Good to Great* (New York: Harper Business, 2001).

Stephen M. R. Covey, *The Speed of Trust* (New York: Free Press, 2006).

Stephen R. Covey, *The 7 Habits of Highly Effective People*, 25th anniversary ed. (New York: Simon & Schuster, 2013).

Angela Duckworth, *Grit: The Power of Passion and Perseverance* (New York: Scribner, 2016).

Carol Dweck, *Mindset: The New Psychology of Success* (New York: Random House, 2006).

Tim Elmore, *Habitudes for Career Ready Students* (Atlanta: Growing Leaders, Inc., 2015).

———, *Habitudes for New Professionals* (Atlanta: Growing Leaders, Inc., 2015).

Marshall Goldsmith, *What Got You Here Won't Get You There* (New York: Hachette Books, 2007).

Carla A. Harris, *Expect to Win* (New York: Avery, 2010).

Michael Hyatt and Daniel Harkavy, *Living Forward* (Grand Rapids: Baker Books, 2016).

Daniel Kahneman, *Thinking Fast and Slow* (New York: Farrar, Straus and Giroux, 2011).

Patrick Lencioni, *The Three Signs of a Miserable Job* (San Francisco: Jossey Bass, 2007).

Crawford Loritts, *Leadership as an Identity: The Four Traits of Those Who Wield Lasting Influence* (Chicago: Moody, 2009).

Greg McKeown, *Essentialism* (New York: Currency, 2014).

Kerry Patterson, Joseph Grenny, Ron McMillan, and Al Switzler, *Crucial Conversations* (New York: McGraw Hill Education, 2011).

Dave Ramsey, *The Total Money Makeover* (Nashville: Thomas Nelson, 2013).

Simon Sinek, *Start with Why* (New York: Penguin, 2009).

Michael Watkins, *The First 90 Days: Proven Strategies for Getting Up to Speed Faster and Smarter* (Brighton, MA: Harvard Review Press, 2013).

Liz Wiseman, *Multipliers* (New York: Harper Business, 2017).

———, *Rookie Smarts* (New York: Harper Business, 2015).

Podcasts

Career Clarity Show, Lisa Lewis, https://podcasts.apple.com/us/podcast/the-career-clarity-show/id1466163000.

Carey Nieuwhof Leadership Podcast, Carey Nieuwhof, https://careynieuwhof.com/mypodcast/.

EntreLeadership, The Dave Ramsey Companies, https://www.entreleadership.com/blog/podcast.

Everybody Matters, Barry Wehmiller, https://www.youtube.com/playlist?list=PLY2mIZkcKLUbRy1O4gG2ITE6uMUo-hCAp.

Happen to Your Career, Scott Anthony Barlow, https://www.happentoyour
career.com/podcast/.

Jenni Catron Leadership Podcast, Jenni Catron, https://get4sight.com/pod
cast/.

Lead to Win, Michael Hyatt, https://michaelhyatt.com/leadtowin/.

Pivot with Jenny Blake, Jenny Blake, http://www.pivotmethod.com/podcast.

School of Greatness, Lewis Howes, https://podcasts.apple.com/us/podcast/
the-school-of-greatness/id596047499.

Personality Assessments/Career Guidance

Birkman Method: Measures interests, behaviors, and needs, https://birk
man.com/the-birkman-method/.

Disc Profile: A tool to understand behavioral differences between people,
https://www.discprofile.com/.

Emotional Intelligence 2.0 Assessment: Measures self-awareness, self-
management, and relationship management, https://www.talentsmart
.com/products/emotional-intelligence-appraisal.php.

Myers-Briggs Type Indicator: Measures introversion or extroversion ten-
dencies, how someone makes decisions, and how a person views others
and the world. The results can help an individual choose a career or
grow in a current role, https://www.myersbriggs.org/my-mbti-person
ality-type/mbti-basics/the-16-mbti-types.htm.

Notes

Chapter 1 Preparing Your Character

1. Carey Nieuwhof, *Didn't See It Coming: Overcoming the 7 Greatest Challenges That No One Expects and Everyone Experiences* (New York: Waterbrook, 2019), 41.

2. Jackie Robinson and Alfred Duckett, *I Never Had It Made* (New York: Golden Springs Publishing, 2016), epilogue.

3. Oprah Winfrey, "Every Person Has a Purpose," Oprah.com, accessed July 7, 2020, https://www.oprah.com/spirit/how-oprah-winfrey-found-her-purpose.

4. "Sir Richard Branson: On a Mission to Mentor," *Motivated* magazine, May 4, 2011, http://motivatedonline.com/sir-richard-branson-on-a-mission-to-mentor/.

5. Peter Economy, "This Is the Way You Need to Write Down Your Goals for Faster Success," *Inc.*, February 28, 2018, https://www.inc.com/peter-economy /this-is-way-you-need-to-write-down-your-goals-for-faster-success.html. See also: "The Science Behind Setting Goals (and Achieving Them)," Forbes-Books, accessed July 7, 2020, https://forbesbooks.com/the-science-behind -setting-goals-and-achieving-them/.

6. Valerie Williams, "Here's an Idea for Breaking the Santa News without Breaking Your Kid's Heart," updated December 15, 2016, https://www.scary mommy.com/viral-post-breaking-santa-news-to-kids/.

Chapter 2 Cultivating Your Competency

1. Robert Iger, *The Ride of a Lifetime: Lessons Learned from 15 Years as CEO of the Walt Disney Company* (New York: Random House, 2019), 5.

Chapter 3 Finding a Job

1. Stephanie Vozza, "Four Reasons Resumes No Longer Work," Fast Company, January 5, 2018, https://www.fastcompany.com/40512551/4-reasons-why-resumes -no-longer-work.

2. Ryan Jenkins, *The Generation Z Guide: The Complete Manual to Understand, Recruit, and Lead the Next Generation* (Atlanta: Ryan Jenkins, LLC, 2019), 249.

Part II Keep a Job

1. Simon Davies, "Career Change Statistics," Careers Advice Online, accessed July 8, 2020, https://careers-advice-online.com/career-change-statistics.html.

Chapter 4 Conquering the First Ninety Days

1. Heather Huhman, "Starting a New Job? Follow the '30-60-90 Day Plan,'" Glassdoor, July 22, 2018, https://www.glassdoor.com/blog/starting-job-follow-306090-plan/.

Chapter 5 Managing Relationships

1. Henry Cloud, *Integrity: The Courage to Meet the Demands of Reality* (New York: HarperCollins, 2006), 17.
2. Stephen M. R. Covey, *The Speed of Trust: The One Thing That Changes Everything* (New York: Free Press, 2006), 13.
3. Stephen R. Covey, *The 7 Habits of Highly Effective People: Powerful Lessons in Personal Change* (New York: Free Press, 1989), 235.

Chapter 6 Managing Your Performance

1. Adunola Adeshola, "How to Get the Feedback You Desperately Need from Your Boss," *Forbes*, April 26, 2018, https://www.forbes.com/sites/adunolaadeshola/2018/04/26/how-to-get-the-feedback-you-desperately-need-from-your-boss/#5ead92822674.
2. Tasha Eurich, "The Right Way to Respond to Negative Feedback," *Harvard Business Review*, May 31, 2018, https://hbr.org/2018/05/the-right-way-to-respond-to-negative-feedback.

Chapter 7 Navigating Land Mines

1. Dee Ann Turner, "Resiliency Is the Antidote for Rejection," *Global Leadership Network*, December 4, 2019, https://nld.globalleadership.org/articles/leading-yourself/resiliency-is-the-anecdote-for-rejection/.

Part III Grow a Career

1. Charlie "Tremendous" Jones, *Life Is Tremendous* (Boiling Springs, PA: Tremendous Leadership, 1968), chap. 4, Kindle.

Chapter 8 Developing Yourself

1. Tony Conrad, "5 Secrets to Finding and Working with a Mentor," *Entrepreneur*, September 23, 2015, https://www.entrepreneur.com/article/250936.

2. Michael Hyatt, "How to Find a Mentor to Help You Go Further, Faster," May 31, 2013, https://michaelhyatt.com/find-mentor/.

3. Alissa Carpenter, "5 Ways Volunteering Can Enhance Your Career," *Forbes*, January 30, 2018, https://www.forbes.com/sites/alissacarpenter/2018/01/30/5-ways-volunteering-can-enhance-your-career/#1d44a9b37962.

4. Justin Miller, president, CARE for AIDS, phone interview with the author, February 13, 2020.

5. Duncan Kimani Kamau, Justin T. Miller, and Cornel Onyango Nyaywera, *Beyond Blood: Hope and Humanity in the Forgotten Fight against AIDS* (Austin: Greenleaf, 2019), 71.

6. Kamau, Miller, and Nyaywera, *Beyond Blood*, 72.

7. Kamau, Miller, and Nyaywera, *Beyond Blood*, 74.

8. "Our Impact So Far," CARE for AIDS, accessed August 11, 2020, https://www.careforaids.org.

9. Iger, *Ride of a Lifetime*, 18.

Chapter 9 Leading Others

1. Napoleon Hill, *Think and Grow Rich* (New York: Chartwell Books, rev. 2015), 100.

2. Daniel Goleman, "Leadership That Gets Results," *Harvard Business Review*, March–April 2000, https://hbr.org/2000/03/leadership-that-gets-results.

3. Marshall Goldsmith, *What Got You Here Won't Get You There: How Successful People Become Even More Successful* (New York: Hatchette Books, 2007), title.

4. Dan Millman, *Way of the Peaceful Warrior: A Book That Changes Lives* (Tiburon, CA: H. J. Kramer, 2000), 105.

5. Kevin Daum, "8 Things Really Great Problem Solvers Do," *Inc.*, September 3, 2014, https://www.inc.com/kevin-daum/8-things-really-great-problem-solvers-do.html.

6. Robbie Bosley, "Square Peg, Round Hole—The Story of Apollo 13," *National Space Centre*, December 4, 2017, https://spacecentre.co.uk/blog-post/story-apollo-13/.

7. Carmine Gallo, *The Storyteller's Secret: From TED Speakers to Business Legends, Why Some Ideas Catch On and Others Don't* (New York: St. Martin's Press, 2017), xix.

8. Rev. A. L. Patterson, "Shamgar," Chick-fil-A, Inc. Annual Conference, Southampton Princess, Bermuda, February 1996.

Chapter 10 Changing Jobs

1. Vivian Giang and Alana Horowitz, "19 Successful People Who Have Been Fired," *Business Insider*, October 19, 2013, https://www.businessinsider.com/people-who-were-fired-before-they-became-rich-and-famous-2013-10.

2. Rachel Gillett, "How Walt Disney, Oprah Winfrey, and 19 Other Successful People Rebounded after Getting Fired," *Inc.*, October 7, 2015, https://www.inc.com/business-insider/21-successful-people-who-rebounded-after-getting-fired.html.

3. Jen Hubley Luckwaldt, "5 Famous People Who Were Fired before Becoming Successful," *The Balance Careers,* November 20, 2019, https://www.thebalance careers.com/famous-people-who-were-fired-2060745.

4. Will Kenton, "Severance Pay," *Investopedia*, updated May 12, 2020, https://www.investopedia.com/terms/s/severancepay.asp.

5. Max Lucado, *You'll Get through This: Hope and Help for Your Turbulent Times* (Nashville: Thomas Nelson, 2013), 3.

Dee Ann Turner is an author, speaker, and thirty-three-year veteran of Chick-fil-A, Inc. Prior to her retirement in 2018, she was Vice President, Talent and Vice President, Sustainability. She was instrumental in building and growing Chick-fil-A's well-known culture and talent systems, and during her long career, she selected thousands of corporate staff and Chick-fil-A franchisees. Today, she leads her own organization, Dee Ann Turner & Associates, writing books, speaking to over fifty audiences per year, and consulting with and coaching companies and leaders globally. Her previous books include *Bet on Talent: How to Create a Remarkable Culture That Wins the Hearts of Customers* and *It's My Pleasure: The Impact of Extraordinary Talent and a Compelling Culture*. She and her husband, Ashley, have been married for thirty-seven years and are the parents of three grown sons. When she is not traveling for business or pleasure, she can often be found on her Peloton bike in Atlanta or stand-up paddleboarding on Lake Hartwell in northeast Georgia. Over the past three decades, she has served on the boards of various organizations and served and led global mission teams. Her life passion is found in Hebrews 12:15: "See to it that no one falls short of the grace of God."

Connect with
DEE ANN

To learn more about Dee Ann's speaking, consulting, and coaching, visit **DEEANNTURNER.COM**

 DeeAnnTurner    DeeAnnTurner

 Dee Ann Turner    DeeAnnTurnerAuthor